IDENTITY, NARCISSISM, AND THE OTHER

IDENTITY, NARCISSISM, AND THE OTHER
Object Relations and their Obstacles

Jean Arundale

KARNAC

First published in 2017 by
Karnac Books Ltd
118 Finchley Road
London NW3 5HT

British Library Cataloguing in Publication Data

A C.I.P. for this book is available from the British Library

ISBN-13: 978-1-78220-397-1

Typeset by Medlar Publishing Solutions Pvt Ltd, India

Printed in Great Britain

www.karnacbooks.com

To
my family, friends, colleagues,
and analysts; and all the "others"
who instate my identity

CONTENTS

ACKNOWLEDGEMENTS

I would like to give warm thanks to my family and friends for their interest, support, and encouragement. My colleagues at the British Psychoanalytic Association have stimulated and informed me over the years in ongoing seminars and discussions, for which I am very grateful. I owe great thanks to supervisors and colleagues at the British Psychoanalytical Society, whose inspiration and example have been invaluable. Without a doubt my analysts, too, have been invaluable and instrumental in every way.

I'm grateful to Karnac Books and Oliver Rathbone for accepting this project. Thanks also to Rod Tweedy, Constance Govindin, Kate Pearce, Kathleen Steeden, Cecily Blench, and the other editors and the publishing team at Karnac for their helpfulness and efficient work.

I would like to give special thanks to colleagues who read various chapters and gave helpful feedback: Lesley Steyn, Julia Sandelson, Victoria Graham Fuller, Ora Dresner, and Karen Nash. Valuable comments and suggestions were given by Ron Britton in regard to Chapters Five and Eight. I owe a particular thank you to Annie Pesskin who went through the final draft and offered helpful editorial recommendations.

Some of these chapters appeared in different incarnations:

Chapter Five, Non-consummation: a narcissistic organisation, was presented to the IPA International Congress in Boston, in July, 2015.

Chapter Six, The other as alien: psychic atopia, was presented at the UCL conference Ron Britton Today, in December 2011.

Chapter Ten, Dreams as access to the primal scene, was published in the *Journal of the British Association of Psychotherapists*, (1989, vol. 15).

Chapter Eleven, Arrested development: notes on a case of paedophilia, was published in *Psychoanalytic Psychotherapy in the Kleinian Tradition*, edited by S. Ruszczynski and S. Johnson (London: Karnac Books, 1999).

I am especially grateful to my patients for sharing with me the absorbing and fascinating work that is psychoanalysis. Our journeys together have been a privilege and a vital learning experience.

ABOUT THE AUTHOR

Jean Arundale is a training and supervising analyst for the British Psychoanalytic Association (BPA) and the British Psychotherapy Foundation (BPF). In the BPA, she served for five years as Chair of the Scientific Committee and member of the Board and has served on various other committees. With a main focus on clinical work in psychoanalytic private practice, she also works part-time as a consultant psychotherapist in the NHS heading a psychoanalytic psychotherapy service at Guy's Hospital, London. After gaining a first degree in philosophy and mathematics, she completed a PhD in psychology at University College London (UCL). She has presented papers at UCL and the European Psychoanalytical Federation conferences, and at the IPA Congress in Boston, and has taught, supervised, published, and edited variously in the field of psychoanalysis.

INTRODUCTION

This book will speak to colleagues and students of psychoanalysis as well as the general reader and those seeking psychoanalysis for themselves. There is a sense in which Chapter One stands apart from the rest in that it delineates how psychoanalysis works to develop a resilient sense of self and reliable identity. Chapter One is intended to introduce major psychoanalytic concepts that can be brought to bear on the establishment of identity, while the following two chapters address the issues of narcissism and the other. The remainder of the book takes up different aspects of psychoanalytic work as they bear on relationships and obstacles in relating. As I am principally a clinician, the emphasis in this book is on case studies and clinical work, though I bring in relevant theoretical scaffolding.

Why, you might ask, is the term "identity" featured, instead of the more usual "self", "sense of self", or perhaps "personality", "character" or "being oneself"? In my view, from moment to moment we are, by turns, gaining, losing, and regaining as we throw ourselves into things, lose ourselves, and recover. Identity is connected with self but implies more stable structures, a network of ideas and mental entities that underpin the whole individual, involving belief systems, principles, and conscience. Identity includes the executive functions of the ego, the manner in which we act and do things, our thinking and emotional patterns springing from memories, aspirations, desires, and identifications with others, all of which operate at both conscious and unconscious levels. These may be aspects of personality that we want to encourage or wish to eliminate. Existing also, as part of us, are the deeper unconscious phantasies that may control us without our knowing; all of these make us who we are. "Having an identity" implies knowing oneself and having an authentic existence rooted in the body, in one's own skin, and centrally in one's mind, to which we return after excursions into the world and into relationships with others. In this book I will, perhaps idiosyncratically, use self, identity, and self-identity interchangeably, for convenience.

While it is possible for your identity to be stolen by online thieves, ironically a personal identity is not so mobile; it cannot be ordered up from the internet or chosen from the shelves of a self-help bookshop. There are biological and genetic constraints emanating from what may be considered a core self, or what Bion described as invariants—those enduring elements of personality that appear in changing forms, that are illusive, mostly unknown, and discovered by intuition (Bion, 1970, p. 41; Vermote, 2011, pp. 362–363). When the patient is introduced to himself, he may find he is not who he thinks he is. However, while we are not self-made, nor self-authored as such, we do have choices in the matter, albeit choices that need to be linked to roots in the internal world, intuited, linked to reason, and tempered. Although self-identity is, according to Bollas (see Nettleton, 2015), like a basic fingerprint, it is one that can develop and grow, to include hopes, intentions, and imaginings about the future. In all of us there is poetry, humour, music, play, philosophy, knowledge, interests, skills, many of these possibly unconscious. Gender, sexual, racial, or national identity are important for many, while identity politics and political movements may be attempts to seek and find self-identity, genuine or spurious. Psychoanalysis may reveal the importance of group identities and much more, but primarily it is the unique individual identity that is the issue.

* * *

Over many years of practising psychoanalysis, three central themes have shown themselves to be recurrent or ubiquitous in every analysis: first, issues around **identity**, involving the struggle to know the self, to understand the self, to accept the self, and to be the self in an authentic way. Identity means knowing who one is, being present in time and space, knowing one's mind and what one believes and stands for. The process of analysis as a way towards finding, integrating, and consolidating an identity will be addressed in Chapter One. The second theme, intricately entangled with identity, is the problem of **narcissism**, viewed in psychoanalytic theory as a defensive retreat to a mental state characterised by an unconscious belief in the special value of the self and the diminution of others. As relationships with **others** are the third central preoccupation in analysis, it is obvious how narcissism in the personality can jeopardise good relationships and stand in the way between the self and the other. People with narcissistic disorders are, by definition, self-involved and have difficulty with relationships.

Human relations for all of us are not easy; there are a multitude of anxieties surrounding closeness and intimacy, as well as distance and separation, a complexity of different factors: traumas from the past, innate factors of hostility to objects, emotional and physical issues such as threats to the integrity of the self, fears of being hurt, taken over, abandoned, betrayed, or annexed by the other. The "urge to merge" poses difficulties in relating to another as a separate person. Chapter Two will interrogate the notion of otherness itself. I will discuss the necessity for the presence of the other in order to recognise and to become a self, in the dialectical process that forms both self and other. The question of otherness has not been as fully addressed in British psychoanalytic theory as it has in French psychoanalysis and I think more attention to it could yield benefits.

These three important themes: identity, narcissism, and the other, are actually so interconnected that it may be a false distinction to divide them, yet I find it helpful to consider each in turn. Let us put it this way: for the person undergoing psychoanalysis there is an expectation that he will discover or rediscover a resilient self and a sense of personal identity. Further, that he will overcome narcissism sufficiently to be able to form good relationships. Among the qualities necessary for us to live with and around others, it is proposed that the essential requirement is empathy, that is, to be able to enter into the mind of the other to experience what it is to be them; connecting with them and experiencing their "otherness", their differences and similarities, with the intention of understanding and relating to them.

The psychoanalytic process is singularly positioned to aid self-discovery, to accomplish what Bion proposed to be its purpose: "to introduce the patient to himself". It is incredible how much of what we do and how we are is unconscious; we sleepwalk our way through life unless we struggle to be self-aware. The method of free association can reveal the self by thinking about feelings and feeling the emotions linked to thoughts; as Wagner said of music, that it emotionalises the intellect, psychoanalysis uses free association to do the same work: to connect thought and feeling, to increase the capacity to tolerate affect and to feel more emotionally alive, to uncover unconscious beliefs and emotional patterns, to identify needs, excavate unconscious aspirations and nascent desires, and thereby release the mind's freedom and creativity.

Complicating and confounding this process may be traumas from the past, grievances, or disturbed and disturbing psychic patterns that come to the fore to invade the present. These must be dealt with and worked through as much as possible—a significant part of every analysis. These fundamentals of psychoanalytic practice will be assumed to be in the background and feature specifically in the foreground of chapters in this book. The psychoanalyst's task of analysing each aspect of a person's mind and character as it arises and accrues, dreams, enactments, phantasies, associations, slips, and parapraxes, the particularities of the unconscious, are shown as ongoing processes in the clinical material of this book.

The problem of narcissism appears to be a preoccupation in present-day psychoanalytic books, articles, and discussions, not only the use of it as a defence, but as libidinal or destructive phenomena that create havoc in the personality. To quote Rosenfeld, a psychoanalyst who studied narcissism in depth: "In considering narcissism from the libidinal aspect one can see that the overvaluation of the self plays a central role, based mainly in the idealization of the self" (1985, p. xx). More ordinary instances of narcissism in the individual are found as healthy, realistic self-esteem or as a necessary temporary retreat at times to repair the self from too much otherness.

In a darker register, destructive narcissism (Rosenfeld, 1971) is even more problematic than excessive self-love, involving omnipotent rage and destructiveness against the existence of the envied other. What do we do with destructive narcissists when they pervert the analytic process in ways we often can't detect? When this situation is found in analysis, the question arises: what is the fate of the narcissist who is living without emotional contact with others, without object love and containment, given that self-aggrandisement is ultimately empty and unsustainable and that even narcissists need love? In Chapter Three

I discuss different aspects of narcissistic phenomena. Omnipotence is illustrated in Chapter Four in the presentation of the vicissitudes of a long analysis of a narcissistic/borderline patient. In Chapter Five I describe a defensive narcissistic organisation or psychic retreat in two patients, formed to protect against an unconscious psychotic phantasy. I have tried to show in these chapters on narcissism the difficulties these patients have around negative feelings towards others and the significance and problems produced by the negative transference.

Freud pointed out in *Thoughts for the Times on War and Death* (1915b, pp. 298–299) that even in our most intimate relationships there are elements of hostility and unconscious death wishes. In this paper Freud couples love and hate, anticipating Klein and Bion, by writing: "Nature, by making use of this pair of opposites, contrives to keep love ever vigilant and fresh, so as to guard it against the hate which lurks behind it" (ibid., p. 299). We are all of us made up of good and bad, love and hate. The analytic situation serves as a microscope to focus on difficulties with ourselves and the other and, as such, the relationship between patient and analyst itself can frequently become the problem. As noted by Britton, for many patients, "Being in analysis is a problem; being in the same room; being in the same mental space. Instead of there being two connected, independent minds there are either two separate people unable to connect or two people with only one mind" (Britton, 2015, p. 68). This situation, termed "psychic atopia" by Britton, is discussed with case illustrations in Chapter Six.

The fear of libidinal relationships exists in us all as the fear of being hurt or taken over, possessed or betrayed. Instead of exciting, the call of the other can be overwhelming and something to be avoided. Dependency, need for the other, and attachment, all risk the possibility of abandonment and loss, or fears of merging with the object and losing the self; to deal with these anxieties, defences are erected. Several of the chapters in this book will maintain that, at root, the motive for embedding defensive or narcissistic organisations in the personality is the hidden presence of psychotic anxieties and phantasies.

In Chapter Seven, sexuality in psychoanalysis is discussed and three cases are presented that exemplify erotic transference, together with fear of emotional intimacy and sexual conflict. Patients whose unconscious guilt prevents progress in analysis, who exhibit the so-called "negative therapeutic reaction", are discussed in Chapter Eight. Negative reactions to what might be good, helpful experiences are obstacles to the full expression of identity and open, spontaneous relations to others. Dreams and symbol formation play an important role in the discovery of unknown parts of the self and the emergence of symbols from dreams will be discussed in Chapters Nine and Ten. Chapter Eleven will look at a case of paedophilia, in which development has altogether gone wrong, and in which dreaming played an important part in freeing up the patient.

As earlier noted, I am primarily a clinician and the emphasis in this book is on clinical work. I present the material herewith to show patients in their struggles with intimacy, love, loss, hate, guilt, and reparation, exploring the relationship between identity, narcissism, and the other. Reading idealist philosophy and philosophy of mind, along with mathematics, at university has inevitably shaped my thinking and way of analysing concepts and patients, for better or worse. I became intrigued by Kant and Hegel, and interested in the Continental philosophers and the existentialists, all of whom take up the study of the self and the mind. For me, the influence of and great love for the Socratic dialogue have been happily transformed into those for the psychoanalytic dialogue— quite a different thing, but both eminently truth-seeking. My patients, partners in the psychoanalytic journey, have taught me a great deal. I have changed the patients' details to protect their identities, in the interests of confidentiality. Throughout the book, I use the conventional spelling "fantasy" to refer to conscious notions and "phantasy" or its close derivatives when the idea is unconscious.

CHAPTER ONE

The way to identity: an auspicious method?

A robust "sense of self" or self-identity is not a given; there are many ways the self can be lost, deformed, split into parts, or falsified. If one is fortunate, a central identity is formed through the vicissitudes of growing up from infancy into adulthood, meeting each stage as it comes, withstanding the developmental challenges and inevitable traumas that occur. Psychoanalytic theory, begun with Freud and developed by Klein, Winnicott, and many others, provides a coherent roadmap of human development, firmly based on a theory of mind, applicable as a method of treatment for a range of disorders, as well as providing an abundant and rich catalogue of difficulties on the journey to an "identity".

Psychoanalysis is particularly suited to the task of finding or refinding the self and establishing an identity if that has not developed or has been lost, fragmented, or become unreal. Some of the pitfalls in establishing self-identity that will be addressed in the chapters of this book will include battles between conflicting parts of the self, splitting the self into parts, excessive projection of parts of the self into others or introjection of parts of others into the self. There can be a surfeit of identifications, playing out roles assigned by parents, or performing other roles that aren't authentic. Feeling oneself to be unreal or false,

1

estranged or out of touch with oneself, or disconnected from others, is discomfiting, to say the least.

So what does psychoanalysis have to offer in establishing an identity? In the first instance, it offers a place to reflect on experience and particularly self-experience, a space to focus on internal psychic reality and to discover meaning, a space in the analytic setting and in the analyst's mind to project and process emotional pain, malaise, or disturbing questions; to understand and to think about oneself; to put words to emotions and to find one's values and what one believes in, one's ambitions, and aspirations. In the unconscious are hopes, intentions, and imaginations about the future, in a constant dialectical relationship between the conscious and the unconscious.

The capacity to reflect on experience can be a neglected skill or perhaps never achieved, but it is important. Research by Fonagy et al. (1991) at the Anna Freud Centre has shown how possession of this capacity in childhood, probably but not necessarily fostered by the mother, affords a degree of resilience against the damage of neglect or trauma. The first clinical vignette I will present below is of a man who began analysis having entirely lost the capacity to reflect upon his experience and lacking a sense of who he was.

While philosophers may question whether or not the self can actually be said to exist (see Kirshner, 1991), I maintain that it can, and it is free association, the very activity on which Freud originally based psychoanalysis, that activates and creates a self. Free association is the method of allowing spontaneous utterances of feelings, fantasies, thoughts, and beliefs to arise from moment to moment from areas deeper in the mind than might occur in everyday life. Free association can be difficult to do. It is the business of allowing oneself to say freely and without purpose whatever comes to mind regardless of the sense or nonsense, the relevance or irrelevance of the utterance. It is not as easy as it might seem to speak without filtering. It requires letting go of control and the strict requirements of logic and reason. Some patients characteristically resist giving themselves over to it (Joseph, 2005). Abraham (1919) observed that certain patients, notably narcissists, find it difficult to expend themselves on free associations, to actually put themselves into the process. Requesting the analysand to free associate sets up a tension between his wanting to explore his unconscious and an opposing force that resists knowing. The analyst's task is to enter the ring, to engage with the patient, to understand and interpret what is going on; the patient's task is to attempt to be as honest as possible. As he listens to the patient, the analyst practices a special kind of listening, "free-floating attention", waiting for the unconscious to speak. The analysand may experience anxiety in the face of the unknown, fears of judgement or censure or losing his bearings or losing control, so that his unconscious resistances will need to be worked with and modified. Analytic patients are evasive; they can begin on an associative train and veer off when they sense something ahead that is not to their liking, throwing the analyst off the trail. It is in the subtleties of free association that the unconscious is intimated and its patterns can be discerned. In the analytic dialogue the analyst is trying to meet with the patient's unconscious, linking with unknown parts of the self, thus working to establish a more authentic and whole sense of self or identity.

As the patient tells the story of his life, together with the ever constant work to overcome resistances to free association and self-reflection, the stage is set upon which the work of analysis is conducted and can deepen. Psychoanalysis, it must be said, is not a method to reconstruct the past in and for itself, to create a narrative and fill in the gaps of memory, as Freud first suggested, but rather a unique method of interaction between patient and analyst in the present time, in the here and now, in which the capacity for emotional contact will be found and developed. A growing focus in the analytic dialogue on what is happening in the room between the patient and analyst allows both to feel more anchored and connected, while also relating to the patient's everyday life and past history, both of which are present in the background and held in mind. Observing the movements in the patient's mind and what they mean constitute the analytic work.

Important keys to developing a sense of identity are rooted in unconscious beliefs and phantasies that emerge in the analytic process. Beliefs are ideas that are held to be true until they are examined, held up to scrutiny, judged or tested as true or false, and then kept or discarded. Similarly, fantasies will need to pass the reality test. To clear the mind of outworn beliefs and psychic debris is part of the process. It must be said, a stable, once-and-for-all establishment of a self-identity is clearly a fiction, as the constantly shifting network of associations, emotions, and thoughts, like a kaleidoscope, are context-dependent and are related to the nature of the object relations activated; the self is approximate yet known through an act of recognition or intuition, a perception that "this is me or mine", integrated in the process of the analytic work. Out of the melange appears the outline of the individual's unique identity.

The analytic process is formative of identity but inevitably in this process past selves will appear, will interfere and colour the present; the patient's associations will bring up memories, traumas, or repeating patterns from the past that will need attending to. Processing the spectres of painful experiences and disturbances from the past, as well as being able to value good, helpful experiences, are an important part of the analytic process. In my view, the past exists in the present in the form of the patient's internal world of objects, the others in one's life, past or present, alive in the here and now; past experiences with others or past selves appear and animate or haunt the present. Links with the past and the future, where we come from and where we are going, are certainly part of our identity, but only the present time is alive with potentiality for contacting the self. We need to be aware of the past and the future but not to live in them, aware as if through a permeable wall, a window or a partly opened door, with no necessity to enter unless something intrudes, asking for our attention. The present, the here and now, is our workroom where thinking, linking, and associating takes place, connecting with elements of identity and the other.

The analytic process evolves through the medium of the transference, which was Freud's (1912b) ingenious discovery of the way we relate to others in the present by unconsciously repeating patterns of relationships from the past. Klein termed the transference "memories in feeling", communicated to the analyst by means of projection, consisting of hidden, unconscious scenarios from the near or distant past, or from the current relationship with the analyst. A paper by the Sandlers (1987) on the present and the past unconscious, interpreted in the relationship to the analyst, is a helpful way of viewing the often chaotic projections and of discriminating the present from the past. Regarding technique, Klein held that before linking with the past or with extra-transference material, first the emotional pattern should be apparent in the present in relation to the analyst. Klein was clear that a complete interpretation consists of linking the transference with the past and with current life in a back-and-forth interplay to reveal the "total situation" (Klein, 1952, p. 54–56).

Mr P

The first clinical material I would like to present is from the opening stages of Mr P's analysis, as he learned to self-reflect and free associate.

Mr P was a man in his forties who had spent the majority of his life aiming at professional success and achieving a top position in his demanding profession, leaving him too busy to reflect on or pay any attention to himself. Instead he had developed a collection of activities and routines that he carried out in an automatic way to deal with relationships and daily life, and that excluded all but the minimum of his own needs and desires. Centred on pleasing and seeing to the needs of his various family members, his current girlfriend, and his clients at work, submitting to their wishes, he operated principally at an unconscious level. It emerged that he believed, omnipotently, that he was responsible for everyone in his extended family, that only he could look after them, and keep them alive. For example, he spoke to his parents several times a day, sorted out their problems, large and small, and travelled home each weekend to make sure they were all right, while covertly enjoying his mother's solicitous care. He left to his girlfriend the conduct of their limited social life and free time, while he looked forward to going back to work on Monday to more of his fourteen-hour days. Identifying with a selfless mother, who gave herself over to the needs of the family, and a workaholic father, he had no sense of self and gave no thought to his own individual needs; he was completely spilt between a brilliantly capable work self and a social self that was, as he told me, "emotionally retarded" and out of touch, which I felt in the transference as an absence of emotional connection. Having no notion of what he wanted for himself, other than a vague idea of wanting a family, he focused on what others wanted, so that it was excruciating for him to make decisions of any kind, especially whether or not to marry. His omnipotence had been given a large knock when a family member became seriously ill and he could do nothing to help, and he had retreated to bed with an overpowering depression in the months before contacting me.

Mr P took to free association readily and felt surprise when his self-reflections showed he was out of touch with himself and had no idea of who he was or what he felt or wanted. He felt shocked by this. He recalled a time in his childhood when this was not the case, when he had had a sturdy sense of who he was, could have fun, even, at times, be naughty and not so compliant. As he began to speak of his feelings, I could see what a very sensitive man he was, so vulnerable to being hurt that he had withdrawn from emotional contact with women after his first girlfriend of three months at university had left him. He had been heartbroken and had shut off from his emotions, and he did not allow himself to feel deeply or to fall in love with any of his subsequent girl-friends. He went through the motions but didn't really let them in, and he had never lived with a woman. Not having noticed before starting analysis that there was anything very awry in him, Mr P became aware that he was observing himself from a distance, as if outside himself. He illustrated this by noting that when he awoke in the morning he found himself saying, "Someone is getting up," or thinking, "Someone is hungry." He was shocked to see that he had become a spectator to his own life, not a participant.

In the analytic relationship, his attempts to please me were immedi-ately apparent and I interpreted this to him, along with examining with him what he actually felt about each association that he brought up. As he got more in touch with his feelings, he began to see that he felt no plea-sure in his life; it was as if he had given up on himself. He soon became aware of a consistent underlying anger that plagued him. He asked him-self: Why was he always doing things he did not enjoy or want to do? Why did he feel he constantly had to please others? In the transference, I pointed out the sense I had that he came to sessions to please and to look after me, instead of focusing on himself. As I began to speak about his needs and his belief that he didn't have a right to a life of his own, he began to wonder about lost parts of himself and what he wanted; he made space to think about what his spontaneous feelings might be, inside and outside the sessions. He said, "I don't want to be told what to do like all my girlfriends have done in the past; I've always gone along with things. If I could say 'no' I wouldn't be so worried about the future." He was sure he wanted to have children but the thought of marriage, which was what all his girlfriends had wanted and his present girlfriend was pressurising him to do, put him into a quandary about what he felt, terrified of making a mistake and marrying the wrong woman. This was a central, conscious conflict that had brought him into analysis but was only the tip of the iceberg of his unconscious beliefs and patterns.

Mr P's compliant transference, brought into play as a repetition of past relationships, entailed agreeing with whatever I said and telling me what he thought I wanted to hear, which I pointed out frequently. As I said how he found it hard say "no" to me when he didn't agree, how it appeared that he was afraid I would become annoyed with him if he dis-sented from my views, he began to question his automatic compliance with my views or his girlfriends' plans (a situation that quite suited her) and to think about his own needs and desires and how they might be negotiated. He told me, "I put too much weight on what others think and I lack belief in my own judgement, so I must think about myself and just get on and do things." As I reflected on his neglect of himself, he said, "I don't know why I haven't thought of these things before. I have avoided knowing who I am all my life, avoiding anything difficult, putting things off." I understood that the passivity he displayed in his emotional life, which was linked to how he avoided making choices and tended to procrastinate, was due to his lack of a firm identity and the capacity to reflect on experience.

In one session Mr P told me, "Suddenly I had an image of what I wanted to do and I texted ten friends I haven't seen for years to ask to meet for a drink, and booked five of them." He was delighted at how much he enjoyed seeing them. He began to look forward to weekends; to slow down from his usual frenetic pace and take walks around London. He decided with difficulty, wrestling with many pros and cons, to go with colleagues to a conference on the Continent instead of following his girlfriend's wishes, as usual, and was amazed at what a good time he had. He took his girlfriend to the opera, negotiating the choice with her for the first time, beginning to speak up for himself instead of retreating into passivity.

Through encountering himself and his analyst, Mr P began to see himself differently; he had begun to question his fixed position and incorporate a new view of himself, my thoughts of him. He appeared to enjoy the process of self-reflection, of finding himself and different aspects of his identity, re-finding his emotions, his needs and desires. However, my attempts to connect with him in the transference at this early stage were deflected or denied as he kept his distance. An example of this was my interpretation that he, while valuing my comments, kept himself apart and ignored my presence, as if I were a function not a person. This led me to believe his compliance was superficial and a case in point of the way he dealt with others: keeping them separate and apart while he got on with his own purposes. This reflected the way in which he split off his emotional life from his professional work, keeping his emotional life barren and going his own way in conducting his rich professional life. This, and other moments when he would brush off my comments summarily, wanting to be in charge of the work, showed me the arrogant and omnipotent aspects of his identity that he hid from himself as much as anyone else.

As I attempted to take up what he felt towards me, and particularly aspects of negative transference, he would respond with varieties of idealisation, such as: "Oh, I think you're great. You're wonderful. I used to pour scorn on therapy; I was against coming and only got in touch with you two years after I got your contact details, when I was *in extremis*. Therapy has been mind-expanding; it doesn't give solutions but gives the wish to find one's own. It's not rocket science but it is something intriguingly clever." This showed to me that idealisation of his object was linked to his ideal self, the two of us doing something clever together, echoing his idealised relationship with his adored, clever, perfect mother who met his every need. No woman could measure up to her and he was startled when he realised he was waiting to meet a woman like his mother before he could marry. In idealising his mother, all of his aggression was split off and expressed in his highly charged career; however, signs of anger towards his mother began to appear as he could see her part in clinging to him and keeping him a child, in her harsh punishments when he was little, and in her ferociously aggressive arguments with his father that frightened and disturbed him, putting him off marriage. Accompanying awareness of his anger was a great amount of anxiety around possibly hurting her or displeasing her, the adored mother he so ardently protected.

Anxiety and aggression

Crucial to being human is the capacity to deal with anxiety, not to simply get rid of it by repression or splitting and projection, and a crucial function of the analytic process is to enable patients to bear, contain, understand, and modify their anxiety. Klein (1932) believed that dealing with anxiety was the greatest task in the development of the child, never fully achieved, and she maintained that the main purpose in analysis was to focus on and interpret the greatest anxiety, the "point of urgency", at any given moment. When the patient's very worst fears are put into words, it is felt they can be faced, appraised as to their reality, and understood. This serves to bring attention to and to "resolve a certain quantity" of anxiety (Klein, 1932, p. 51), from the past, present, or future, including anxiety arising due to the analytic situation itself. Klein demonstrated how the sojourn of conscious and unconscious anxieties as they pass through the mind of the psychoanalyst calms and restores the patient on the journey to identity.

Mr P's greatest anxiety was that his parents would die: he hadn't accepted that this was inevitably going to happen at some point, a fact of life. This and the other sources of his anxiety, the frightened child, the angry son unable to marry, the descent from omnipotence into helplessness and retreat to bed, were uncontained and overwhelming to him. Entering analysis, Mr P found the containment he needed to be able to think about his anxiety and himself. Containment is Bion's (1962) concept based on the mother/infant model that plays a vital role in psychoanalysis, the way in which the mother takes in, holds in mind, and modifies the "nameless dread" projected by the infant, returning it in a less toxic form. Bion's model of the container/contained stimulated and furthered the development of theories of projective identification, that is, the way parts of the self are put into the other to disown and get rid of them. The setting and the analyst's mind offer a place of receptivity and containment, where there is a capacity to take in communications of all kinds and to think about them with the patient. Without a functional container to receive projections, there is no place to modify an internal object that is bad/sad/mad/absent/rejecting/ideal/denigrated; without containment there is no place to express and repair a broken love.

Our identities are formed fundamentally by our object relations, the various other people in our lives and the qualities of relationship with them, particularly those whom we have loved or hated. The term "object" is used in psychoanalysis as a neutral technical term to denote the other, indeterminate of whether it is inside or outside, past or present, in reality. The internal object is an image of the other taken into the mind, partly realistic and partly characterised by aspects of the self projected into it. As the patient's internal world of objects emerges along with feelings, phantasies, and beliefs about these objects, their meaning and status can be perceived and their reality examined. They may be lost to the patient, and require mourning. They may be distorted and need modifying, or if they are damaged, amends may be initiated. Work in the transference, particularly the negative transference, has a significant part to play in the restoration and reparation of internal objects. By means of empathy, the analyst enters into the patient's internal world (Sohn, 1998), moving about, feeling, observing, thinking, practising a particular kind of listening to the state of the patient's objects, identifying with them to gain understanding of each relationship, many aspects of which may be unconscious to the patient, as were Mr P's towards his mother. Through understanding and analysis of the emotional colouring and unconscious phantasy contained in internal object relationships, the patient and analyst may arrive at understanding essential aspects of the patient's identity.

Below, I will discuss another patient, Rosie, whose analysis had deepened over a long period and demonstrated a split in her identity, which could be seen in her love and hate in the transference. In normal infant life, the infant's love for the mother and her nurturing breast is split apart from hatred for the mother who is unreliable or absent, separating them to protect the goodness of the breast; this may be replicated by the patient in analysis as it was with Rosie. Klein (1935, p. 270–271) emphasised the importance of the guilt the infant feels when he discovers that the good mother who feeds and cares for him is the same as the bad mother who is inevitably at times absent, who engenders feelings of rage, starvation, or persecution. As the infant developmentally begins to have the capacity to sustain psychic experience, he begins to experience the mother as a whole object, not completely good or bad, but "good enough", reliable enough, and, because she is no longer split into only good and only bad, she appears more real to the infant. Klein built on Freud's basic understanding of the analytic situation as drawing on and arousing the same underlying process of mother/infant interaction: of separation and reunion, of nurture and feeding, where fears and terrors are transformed into bearable anxiety, and this process fosters the joining together of split-apart love and hate.

Klein outlined the crucial role played by infant oral sadism, that is, the instinct to bite, to chew, to swallow, and destroy in phantasy the goodness of the breast and the mother. It is remorse about this destructiveness that is the foundation of all our good human qualities: concern, care, gratitude, love, and kindness. The development of the ego and our sense of self, on which our integrity and love are based, are due to the transformation of sadism into love, through the capacity to experience guilt and reparation. This stage of development is known in the Kleinian tradition as the depressive position. It was the illuminating insight of Melanie Klein to recognise and conceptualise within psychoanalytic theory the importance of remorse, reparation, and gratitude. She and many others have shown evidence for the way in which unconscious guilt in the struggle between love and hate are responsible for disturbances in the psyche and in relationships, often preventing the person from finding an identity, enjoying life, or making progress in analysis. This problematic situation will be addressed fully in Chapter Eight, describing the situation in which unconscious guilt stands in the way of therapeutic change. Guilt arises in connection with the fear that unconscious destructive impulses have attacked and damaged the very people who are most loved. For Klein (1940), making reparation is a fundamental element in love and all human relationships. To my mind, Klein's emphasis on the notion of reparation stands out importantly among her many contributions to the field of psychoanalysis, resounding, too, in the general culture.

The conscience or superego plays the role of internal arbiter in matters to do with guilt and reparation, and is discussed in regard to many of the patients in these chapters. A strong superego can be a good internal object that structures the mind or it can be punitive and cruel, destructive of the self and the ego (O'Shaughnessy, 1999). When there is a savage critic within, there can be paralysis of the ego's ability to decide or to act. When, in order to preserve the self, the severe critic is turned against others, relationships wither.

In the process of analysis, as we "introduce the patient to himself", for self-identity to be fully realised it is necessary to know both the good and bad parts of the self, to own up to unwanted, undesirable aspects such as jealousy, envy, sadism, or destructiveness, as well as to be able to own one's goodness and positive attributes and achievements. When we become aware of undesirable patterns, there can perhaps be a choice. In taking up elements of inbuilt aggression, equal weight needs to be given to love and reparation in a climate of humanity and understanding (Brenman, 2006). Our sense of well-being comes from being able to internalise and preserve good objects through love. For identity and stability, having a good object inside is crucial.

Rosie

The second patient I will present in this chapter is Rosie, whose excessive anxiety and aggression, split and scattered self-representations, along with other factors, prevented her from being herself. Rosie's material illustrates something of the journey of finding the self, a longer view of the vicissitudes of work with a patient whose analysis eventually brought insight and a sense of self-identity.

Rosie was a vivacious, bright, pretty, young woman, with a serious, idealistic side to her as well as a lively sense of fun. Her parents were hippies, unmarried, who separated when she was very young. She slept in mother's bed until she was fifteen, hating it, full of shame, yet having panic attacks when alone in her own bed. Not wanting to admit to herself how frightened she was, she kept up the illusion that it was her mother who needed her by her side, and indeed mother did not try to encourage her to sleep in her own room. Throughout her childhood, mother spoke to Rosie about her own problems and fears, seeking comfort. Thus, mother and daughter clung to each other, merged claustrophobically, each so identified with the other that neither had a separate identity. It was clear from the beginning that Rosie needed analysis to find herself. Her identification and fusion with her mother had obscured her own identity. I will attempt to give a flavour of the six-year, four-times-weekly analysis, to outline how her selfhood developed.

Rosie's separated parents created a terrible dichotomy in her life as a child. On her much desired but irregular visits to her father, who kept an intermittent contact, she would feel immensely guilty about leaving her mother at home alone, and for secretly yearning to be a child in her father's new family. Her parents hated each other, so she felt disloyal to each when she was with the other, feeling she was a different person, and not herself, when she was with either of them. In spite of her interdependency with her mother, Rosie did manage to leave home and go to college, but she experienced a great deal of guilt about separating from mother. At college, she isolated herself, had panic attacks, and did not do well either academically or socially. Bewildered about what to do with her life, and certain she would not be able to have a relationship with a man or to earn her own living without help, she started analysis, at first three, then four, times a week. It wasn't long before she found a boyfriend, Ken, with whom she replicated the merged, angry relationship with her mother.

In the early sessions, Rosie's intense anxiety suffused the sessions, permeating all her associations, which came in repetitive fragmented cycles, and in the countertransference I too felt fragmented and in pieces, trying to keep up with her and make contact. There appeared to be no place in her mind that was calm and safe, where she could think with any possibility of coherence without the intrusion into and interruption of her mind by irrational phantasies, doom-laden thoughts, or anxious irrelevant meanderings. I understood this fragmentation to be a defence against allowing close contact with me, and it soon became clear that it was her anger and aggression towards her objects that she was struggling with. My attempts to get hold of and put into words the source of her anxiety and deep pessimism were pushed away by her insistence that life was impossible for her, that her fears were real and there was nothing that could be done about them. Loudly vocal in her feelings of being a victim, she expressed hatred and anger towards all her objects, feeling badly treated by everyone. She expressed a wish to be left alone, yet at the same time felt desperately in need of relationships. No one, she said, ever gave her what she most wanted, which was to feel desired and loved; instead she was always disliked. She responded to my comments on her feelings with remarks such as: "You don't understand. I don't *feel* that way, that's the way it *is*. Everyone *does* hate me. I'm sure you hate me too." She maintained the belief that her feelings were facts, which I consistently pointed out to her. Further, I understood her persecutory beliefs as her projected hatred, her hatred of others that she attributed to them, and that a significant element that prevented her from being herself was that she hated both herself and her objects. I took up her self-hatred and hatred of others in various ways and in the transference as a belief she was not acceptable or liked by me, that at times she hated me, and that she felt she would have to be someone different in order to be loved.

Rosie was scathing in her criticisms of her mother and reported frequent, violent arguments with her. She viciously attacked her boyfriend for not considering her needs, then would admit to me that she was the one who insisted on acting in such a way as to please him and focus on his needs, denying her own. Central to her dilemma around identity was that she had an entrenched belief that unless she did what other people wanted her to do, she would be unacceptable and rejected. At the same time, this enraged her. She believed there was no way to be herself and also be acceptable to others.

Much of the time in the early years, Rosie hated me and tried to pick fights, criticising me and arguing with whatever I said. As this went on and on, I interpreted to her that she felt we could only repeat the past over and over again, the early relationship between an unhappy little girl and a mother who could not satisfy or soothe her. I said that she didn't expect anyone would be able to understand how she felt or to help her, that there was an infant self in her who couldn't make real contact with a mother-analyst. Illustrating her narcissistic dilemma, she took control of the analysis, rejected my attempts to be with her and understand her, and subsequently felt alone and lonely.

Her acute irritation in the sessions could be understood as transference from the situation of being in bed with her mother, hating her with intensity, yet too scared to be alone. My interpretations of this maternal transference, that being with me was like being in bed with her mother, brought back memories, including the recollection of having disgusting dreams that her mother wanted to have sex with her. She related to me that when in bed with her boyfriend, he would often turn into an image of her mother. The maternal transference represented both a wish for safety in bed with her mother/me and an angry disturbing fear of this, a deeply ambivalent phantasy.

The following interchanges in the third year of analysis show Rosie's terrible ambivalence and difficulty in being with others. This material took place after she had started a course of study and Ken had moved back into his own flat during the week.

[Rosie abbreviated as R. Analyst abbreviated as A.]

R: It's so difficult living with Ken; I'd rather live alone. I can't bear to have anyone around when I work. I can't stand them making noise or chewing, particularly chewing gum. When I go into a coffee shop, like today, and see a woman sitting alone at the only available place at a table, I think, oh, why isn't someone else sitting there too? I can't bear just to sit down at her table. I can't stand it. If there were just one other person there, two people, it would be OK, I could sit with them. If someone comes to join me when I'm alone at a table, it feels like they want something from me, that they are watching me.

A: [I understood this to mean that, in the two-person relationship, she tended to merge with the other, to lose herself, to surrender to the demands of the other, both desirable and hateful urges.] When you are here with me you feel I watch you and want something from you.

R: Like I felt in bed with my mother, that she wanted me to have sex with her, all those dreams I had of sex with her. Ugh, yuk.

It's the same with M [a girlfriend], I can't stand to have her phone me. It feels like she wants something, wants to see me, and that if we get close it means I can't have a relationship with Ken. We've talked so much here about how I feel I can't have a relationship with both a man and a woman at the same time, like it was with my mother and father.

A: You feel if you get too close to me, I'll be possessive and won't want you to have a man. It's like your relationship with your mother, feeling she would never let you go, didn't want you to have a relationship with your father or with a man of your own. It is terrible for you to bear being close to her or to me, a fear you will be pulled into a tangled, meshed relationship and not able to feel separate or to feel you are your own person.

R: I see that I often think of you as my mother. Ken says I try to make him into my mother, and he won't let me. But you have to let me, to put up with me. I make everyone into my mother. I'm getting better with her; I don't shout at her anymore, except for the last time I was there. We got on so well for the whole weekend, then at the end I lost it. I'm getting better at separating, I think. I don't think I'll ever shout at her again, or argue.

I feel better when I'm not living with Ken. When we were living in the same house, I would be impossible, especially around the time of my periods, terrible. I would pick fights, argue. I just need my own space; I need to live alone to do my work. I'm better when I don't have Ken to argue and fight with but then that's me just blaming him for everything.

A: It is difficult here in the same room with me, sharing this space, arguing with me, blaming me.

Over the years, the maternal transference would return regularly in many variations as it was worked through: the paranoid/schizoid anguish of fighting off merger and, when she felt separate, the terror of being alone.

Tolerating being herself

Rosie expressed the belief that if only she could please me and be a good patient, not so disagreeable, she would be better. I was attentive to and interpreted the performative aspect of her presentation, alert to when she was saying what she thought I wanted to hear or playing a part, rather than being the person she was. I tried to help Rosie to be authentic in my presence and to feel she had the right to be herself, to be someone separate from her mother and me, and to express whatever was on her mind. In this way, she was offered a place to be herself with someone who accepted what it felt like to be her, in all her illogical contradictoriness, ambivalence, argumentativeness, angry attacks, and emotional lability. I subscribed to the theory that if she felt I could bear her, which was actually quite difficult, she could begin to accept and bear herself. It seemed that as I became interested in her internal world and how her mind worked, she also became curious about herself. As I got to know her, as she heard me think aloud about her, she began to know and be herself.

As I grew to know Rosie better, I became aware of how much of the anger and aggression she felt towards her objects was projected into them, then returned to her in the form of psychotic phantasies, a frightening part of herself she was becoming acquainted with. For example, unpleasant friction with her landlady mushroomed into a scary confrontation, seeing the landlady as an evil witch, and Rosie was panicked when she had to speak to her. Or she would imagine a ghostly presence in her room, or have various terrifying paranoid fantasies and dreams during the night. I viewed these visions as angry phantasies of Rosie and her mother, grotesquely combined and fused. On a Monday in a period in which her boyfriend had been away, she told me how happy she was having the flat all to herself. However, she told me, "Last night I was really scared because I was on my own. I can't win. In bed I woke up and I saw monsters in the large mirror in the bedroom. Of course I saw monsters; there's no way not to see monsters with a wall of mirrors [heavy sarcasm]." I interpreted that I turned into a scary monster on the weekends when she felt I wasn't there to help, that she felt alone, abandoned, and angry with me. She responded, "I *am* alone. My dad is coming to look at flats with me, but he doesn't help. My stepmother pretends to want to help, but she doesn't really." I said that she felt angry that I didn't help her enough. She said, "I'm just pretending to be mad at you. It's not really your job to help me with a flat, but maybe I want to hurt you. Dad and Ken don't help me the way they ought to [she says this bitterly]. Dad was never a dad and Ken is not a good boyfriend."

Joining love and hate

After the bitter remarks above there was an abrupt change of affect, from bad to good: "Dad is coming next week and that's a good thing. I don't know what I'm complaining about, I'm just fucking irritable and hormonal. I had a really good talk on the phone with Ken last night and I miss him. And you are really here for me, more than anybody has ever been." It can be seen in this passage that she was using the analytic space as an area for containment and linking of experiences of love and hate, side by side, absence and presence, aspects that had previously been split apart, in relation to her objects and to me in the transference. This dialectical process, repeatedly experienced, fostered in Rosie a modification of the internal and external bad objects and a strengthening of the internalised good object.

The appearance of guilt and reparation

Sometimes Rosie continued to hate me, to keep a distance, or to attack me, and sometimes she felt very positively towards me, feeling close and grateful for the analysis. There was movement in the analysis as she began to feel guilty and sorry after attacking me. She felt remorseful for having argued with me and for having been unpleasant and ill-tempered, particularly before weekend breaks and holidays. The fact that I didn't retaliate, wasn't destroyed by her attacks, and was still there for her, made her guilt tolerable for her. Comprehending what was going on between us, the transference, enabled her to see that the damage she believed she had wrought on me as her primal object was either phantasy or was reparable, and her self-hatred lessened. As I interpreted in the transference the ways in which she felt that I was her mother, her father, her boyfriend, or friends in unconscious phantasy, and as we worked with her distress and anger around weekends and breaks, her hated, rejecting or fused internal objects were modified. Along with this process was a more conscious external repair, as she tried intentionally and through experience to improve her relationships. Her oedipal love for her father and the crushing disappointment he represented were particularly poignant, and much analytic time was given over to oedipal phantasies and the bitterness of the failure of her oedipal love. In her phantasies of the exciting forbidden pleasures of the Oedipus complex, she had felt pushed out of the Garden of Eden.

As the analysis progressed, it could be observed that Rosie's maternal object was undergoing change and repair. In a session that began with my giving dates I would be away for a two-week break, she was furious and critical that I didn't write down the dates on a piece of paper for her. I wondered why she didn't believe she could remember them herself, containing them in her mind. She said:

R: You always put me in the wrong. You're saying you want me to do it your way. What does it matter?

A: You don't want to even try it my way, to use your mind as a container, which is part of our work that *does* matter. This is linked with the problems you have remembering what we say here, our work together, when you leave the sessions.

R: I will forget. Why can't you just write it down? What the fuck does it matter. I'm fucking angry with you. I'm always wrong in your mind.

A: When I speak to you, asking you to explore something, you twist what I say and feel I blame you and say you are wrong.

There was silence for a minute or two, then she abruptly changed tack, which I attributed to the work done on integrating the bad and good maternal objects:

R: I talked to my mother on the phone. We had a really good talk. I felt she liked me and loved me. I always know she loves me but this time I felt she also liked me. I was very moved. I don't want to get so angry with people. My mother had been to a film festival. She saw a film called *Three Years at Sea*. She is starved of culture. It was a silent black-and-white film of a man who lived alone in the wilderness, with snow all around, very bleak. She loved the film and phoned me to tell me. Loads of people didn't get it, but she did. She was telling me and it broke my heart … [Rosie started to cry].

A: Broke your heart …?

R: We understood each other … [crying].

A: You connected with her. You are happy for your mum. She loved the film, you want her to be happy, she liked you and loved you; you could share something important with her.

R: My mother told me a story of staying in a house with hippies with my dad. It was snowy and cold. It wasn't a cult; she had been in those previously. She talked fondly about that time.

A: That was a time when she and your father were together, when they were in love.

R: Yes, and I know that man in the film, I know exactly what he was feeling, lying in the heather looking at the sky. At one with nature. I told her sometimes I feel like that in London. We were just talking; she was telling me about her life … [pause] Ken's gran is dying. It feels so weird. I'm alone so much of the time, every exchange with anybody is important. I wish I could take back the anger toward you that I felt at the beginning today.

A: You're afraid that you hurt me, that I will hold that anger against you, that I can't let it go, that I won't like you or want you. [I had in mind here the great difficulty she had in letting go of anger along with a fear that she damaged others.]

R: Ken's family are staying up all night.

A: They are holding a vigil, watching over her.

R: [She started to cry again] Ken really cares about his gran. It's so sweet. They are scared for her; she's frightened to die. It makes me think of my mother and when it comes to her time to die.

In this material, Rosie was getting in touch with feelings of love, a sense of the value of others, finding a better relationship with her mother, able to see her as a loved, separate person with a life and feelings of her own, one who would die one day and leave her. In the exchanges in the session, there was recognition of the joining together of her parents in the love and sexual union that produced her, which was reparative given that she had begun her analysis believing her origins were in a primal scene of hatred and war.

As time went on, Rosie and her analyst "lived through" the tumultuous experience of her unbearable emotions. Her analyst was there with her as witness and participant as she acquired the experience of finding herself, discovering what she believed and what she wanted in her life, and crucially, realising that a life was actually possible—that she could choose, intend, and then carry out her intentions.

Discussion

In the account of the opening period of Mr P's analysis, it was possible to see how free association and self-reflection in the analytic process enabled him to begin to be in touch with lost selves or prior identities, lively parts of himself that could not only work hard but could also have fun and feel love. As the analysis progressed, regaining contact with his emotional life meant he could weigh up options and choose what and who he wanted in his life, and could form real relationships with others not based on false compliance. It was an important step when he began to grasp the extent of his belief in his omnipotent power to make things happen, the belief that he alone could protect his family from harm, even death; he began to see himself from a different, human point of view, accepting the facts of life. Mr P had not separated from the nexus of his family, had not given up his special place as oedipal child, nor admitted that his mother could be anything but perfect. As the analysis proceeded he struggled as he recognised her role in his difficulties and his split-off anger towards her.

Rosie was a very different personality, although beset with a similar split between aggression and love. Through the psychoanalytic process, Rosie was able to understand herself better and to become aware of her aggressive phantasy attacks and real attacks on her objects, and to trace the source of her aggression. As hatred and positive affectionate emotions towards her primary object became linked together, her object could be viewed in a more realistic and restored version. In both of the patients discussed, as analysis proceeded their views of their idealised objects, Rosie's father and Mr P's mother, were modified into truer, more realistic versions. Mr P no longer felt his mother was perfect or that he was omnipotent, and his need to check frequently that she was OK, undamaged by his phantasy attacks, diminished.

In his object relations theory, Bion constructed a shorthand to represent the basic links to others and to reality: L, H, and K representing Love, Hate, and Knowledge. By experiencing and linking love and hate, which requires tolerating ambivalence and frustration, it is possible, by means of curiosity, to arrive at K, that is, knowledge of the self and others. I believe Bion was pointing out that strong love and hate act as a disturbance to K, the real relationship with objects and the world. Bion remarked, "It is a part of common experience that strong feelings of love and hate affect ability to discriminate and learn" (Bion, 1965, p. 70). When L and H are exaggerated or cannot be linked together and integrated, K is distorted and falsified.

In Rosie's journey of finding herself, she began to experience her objects as less persecutory and more helpful. Instead of two parents who hated each other, who had to be kept entirely separate, never speaking about one when with the other, she could imagine them at one time as having fallen in love, having sex, and conceiving her. She moved from thinking that her mother was a pathetic, lonely, unmarried, and abandoned figure, whom Rosie felt responsible for, to someone who had friends, work, a community, a social life, and was a person who enjoyed herself, which Rosie discovered to her surprise during visits to her home town. Instead of shouting with rage at her mother, unable to feel either understood or separate, she found she could enjoy talking to her and sharing views. She also got on better with her father, with whom she would regularly speak on the phone and visit, experiencing a less idealised version of him and viewing him more clearly as some-one limited in what he could give her, often depressed, yet interest-ing and interested in her. Her boyfriend, previously idealised or raged against, denigrated as mean or unfair, became a friend and lover, and her constant impulses to break up with him diminished. In the transfer-ence, I became valued as a good object.

Strong feelings of hate, beyond the disturbance of mind and interfer-ence with truth engendered, are felt to damage both the object and the self. The experience of knowing that one is attacking one's good object is devastating and creates powerful guilt. As Rosie became more aware of the anger and hate she felt towards others, her guilt was immense, and this then turned into further outbursts of rage and resentment towards those who caused her to feel guilty. Nevertheless, she began to make attempts to repair her present-day relationships and sometimes her intentions could be carried through. She felt, importantly, remorse for attacks on me, and worked to repair our relationship. Out of the chaos of Rosie's life, her futile attempts to deal with her anxiety and pain through evacuation, pouring out her rage in prolonged rants and repeated enact-ments of the angry mother–daughter relationship, and projecting her hatred of others, feeling hated by them, she slowly over the six-year analysis reached a sense of her own separate identity as a person who could love and wanted to be loved. She then developed plans for her future and went on to implement them.

* * *

Bion famously said that psychoanalysts are ones who have the luxury of viewing emotions as facts, while Nietzsche said there are no facts, only interpretations. Interpretation is the analytic tool that majorly reveals identity through the putting-together of words that reflect what is happening in the room, in the here and now. These interpretations are hypotheses that are tested and reformulated again and again to get to psychic truth.

To be introduced to the self, as Bion suggested, is not to do with the transmission of intellectual knowledge, but is discovered by patient and analyst together through a feelingful, intuitive finding of enduring aspects of the self and "selected facts" as they appear in the analysis (Bion, 1967). These constitute identity as I understand it. Bion introduced into analytic thinking the important sphere of emphasis that learning to know one's own mind constructs a "mind of one's own" and, concomitantly, fosters sensitisation to other minds. With the formation of a mind comes affect regulation, the capacity to think, listen, take in, metabolise, then to apply what has been learned. Bion wrote of the mental processes underlying "learning from experience", which first occur in the analytic setting, and then are instated in the mind to be used in experiences in the external world. He wrote, "… the alpha function during the experience [of analysis] provides the elements needed for model making in a subsequent experience" (Bion, 1962, p. 75). Thus, in Rosie's analytic work of thinking and linking, designated by Bion as "alpha function", new models of herself, new versions of identity in relation to her objects, were created. Furthermore, essential to this work, Bion considered that "… selected facts have to be worked upon by conscious rational processes" (ibid., p. 72), and applied in reality.

The redefinition of identity is worked out internally in psychoanalysis through both subtle and palpable rearrangements, constructions, and inventions in the analytic relationship. The Italian psychoanalysts Diena and Serrati (2008), have written about the function of creativity in the search for identity, the way in which the exploration and knowledge of the self combines with the process of reparation of the inner world of objects in creative recombination and construction to create a unique identity. New self-representations arise in dreams, phantasies, and play as identity is consolidated.

This chapter, with its emphasis on finding the self or identity, may seem to the reader to be something of an apotheosis of the self; however, in the view I represent, it is maintained that selfhood intrinsically involves "the other", our objects compose the fabric of which we are made. When self-identity and separateness are realised, the capacity to be curious about and to know the real other can be inaugurated. The concepts of the other and otherness will be explored more fully in the next chapter.

CHAPTER TWO

Otherness and the other

Consciousness first finds in self-consciousness—the notion of
mind—its turning point, where it leaves the parti-coloured show
of the sensuous immediate, passes from the dark void of the
transcendent and remote super-sensuous, and steps into the
spiritual daylight of the present.

—G. W. F. Hegel (1964, p. 227)

In Freud's beginnings in Vienna as a doctor of neurology who treated
hysterics, there was no indication that he intended to go on to create a
system or theory of mind. Yet, as his thought developed, it is difficult
to believe that he wasn't influenced by the thinking of the great system-
builders of nineteenth-century German philosophy, such as Kant,
Hegel, and Marx, the *zeitgeist* into which he was born. As Freud wrote,
he notoriously contradicted himself and added new ideas that were
not consistent with older ones; however, as he elaborated his models
of the mind, taken as a whole, we can see that his thinking amounts to
a substantial theory of mind, albeit "loosely jointed" (Sandler, 1983).
When the Kleinian development is considered as an integral part of
this system, a valid extension of pre-oedipal theory that I believe to be
consistent with Freud's principles, we are provided with an enriched

model of the mind based on Freud's framework, further elaborated by the many psychoanalytic writers who have followed. Our psychoanalytic heritage amounts to an open system not a closed one, linked to and overlapping with philosophical and psychological systems that study the same phenomena, both an edifice and a quarry, a superstructure of theory and a practice that mines the depths of the unconscious, capable of incorporating new discoveries, which is required if psychoanalysis is to avoid dogma.

Hegel's monumental work, *The Phenomenology of Mind* (1964), is devoted to tracking the development of the self or, as he calls it, "self-consciousness" or mind. It is a book that can also be read in its parallel meaning as a history of culture. The above quote from Hegel shows his concept of the self or mind as becoming activated and real in the "daylight of the present", the here-and-now. Hegel's system is a dialectical theory of how the individual subject is created by means of contact with another self-consciousness, with other selves and otherness. He saw in the self's construction, conflict, deconstruction, and ever-moving shifts in its formation, movements of self in its intense longing to become more fully itself on the way to the Hegelian "absolute" or "spirit" or "truth". This, he stated, is one and the same as "self-identity". Once achieved, there is a return to the beginning as self-identity continues to develop. At every step, "the other" is crucial, just as in psychoanalysis, where we call it "the object".

In this chapter I will attempt to show that Hegel's description of the self and its need for the other in order to exist, is strikingly similar to psychoanalytic thinking, in particular the need for recognition by the other in order to achieve identity. Hegel stated:

> Self-consciousness exists in itself and for itself, in that, and by the fact that it exists for another self-consciousness; that is to say, it *is* only by being acknowledged and "recognized". (1964, p. 229, Hegel's italics)

However, self-consciousness in the view I will represent not only finds itself in a positive moment of recognition by the other, but is formed by a refutation of the other, a negation and repudiation: this other is NOT me. I propose that identity is formed in psychoanalysis by transactions with the other, the analyst, in a process comparable to the Hegelian dialectic, consisting of struggle, negation, and affirmation. That is to say, in reading Hegel in comparison with psychoanalysis, in my view, the Hegelian dialectic and its formation of the self can be seen as essentially the same process as the psychoanalytic notion of projection and introjection, corresponding to the Freud/Klein/Bion idea of how the mind is formed.

The term "projective identification" was coined by Klein in 1946 and was conceived as an aggressive projection of parts of the ego into an external object, in order to dominate, control, and to make it part of the ego. Klein did not elaborate on this concept, but many others have done so, using projective and introjective identification as a model for the basic mechanisms of human interaction. (See Sandler [1987] for a critique of the concept.) The process described is one in which the subject splits off and projects aspects of itself into the object, identifying with the other and at the same time taking back and re-introjecting into itself the new version of self that has been recognised, the projection that has been changed and enhanced, suffused with desirable elements of the other while denying and negating their existence in the other. This operation is a powerful mental operation that transforms the self and the other. It is often forceful and manipulative, and, when under its influence, the subject is highly affected. It gives rise to confusion between self and other, a struggle to distinguish "me" from "not me", sometimes evoking a violent negation of the other and an insistence on its own version of itself. Thus, the ego develops itself in opposition to what it is not and also what it wants to be.

One of the few psychoanalytic writers who has shown an interest in Hegelian dialectics is Mills (2000), who discusses projective identification in depth as the process underlying all mental activity. He describes how the projection of parts of the ego into the object has the aim of "dominating or consuming" in order to make the contents part of its own constitution, cancelling opposition, and at the same time maintaining and preserving it as part of a higher mental organisation, synthesising and invigorating the mind in its own progressive thrust towards becoming itself. In other words, projective identification is the fundamental ontological factor or mental structuring process of dialectical progression: the initial negation of an opposite before taking it into the mind. Mills makes interesting comparisons between Hegel and Bion on phantasy and the thinking function. He also makes the interesting point that Hegel did not coin the phrase "thesis-antithesis-synthesis"; this formulation was Fichte's and not actually Hegel's.

Dialectical theories are looked upon with suspicion in British scientific discourse, which is rooted in the empirical and natural science traditions. Nevertheless, the concept of projective and introjective identification has been taken up widely in British psychoanalysis, and its similarity to the Hegelian dialectic is interesting and undeniable. When Rosenfeld stated "… identification by projection and introjection usually occur simultaneously" (1965, p. 171), something that Spillius said is now recognised by most Kleinian analysts (Spillius et al., 2011, p. 60), he was describing a dialectical mental process in which a moment of recognition creates both subject and object as they exist in relation to each other. Neither can be realised in isolation; they are interdependent and made up of each other. Infant and mother, pupil and teacher, spouses, friends, patient and analyst, we are all composed of the other's projections that have been ultimately accepted and integrated. In spite of various uses that projective identification might be put to—and there are many, for example, communication, acquisition, defensive uses such as evacuation, omnipotent control, colonisation, an attempt to get the object to enact unconscious aims, or constituting a destructive attack—the process is basically the action of mind-building. Projective identification, which is then taken back into the subject and introjected, "is the foundation on which normal development rests" (Bion, 1967, p. 103). Thus, Hegel was a forerunner of Klein's and Bion's theories, studying the same phenomenon: the process of the creation of the mind and the self, the struggle to determine who's who and what is true, that is, the process of projecting into the other, negation of the other, then returning to itself, combining and reuniting, creating a new version of identity. I understand that it is through the work of sorting out projective identifications that the self is manifested in its thrust towards a personal identity.

Hegel described the forcefulness that takes place in the dialectical process when there is cancelling of the other "self-consciousness", to be free of it, taking it into the ego as oneself, in order to be oneself and find one's truth, (Hegel, 1964, p. 232). As "pure negation", destruction at the same time preserves and maintains what is destroyed at a meta-level. I understand this to mean that at an unconscious level the other is obliterated, its desirable contents taken in as its own—usurped—while, simultaneously, the undesirable element is forcefully refuted and refused entry into the ego. In the psychoanalytic process, this means an instinctive repudiation of the hated, disowned, or feared parts of the self, putting them into the analyst. This presents problems for the clinician, who needs to be able to take in the often powerful and disturbing projections, process them and return them to the analysand. The aim in analysis is to return unbearable experiences and destructive projective identifications in a more tolerable and acceptable form, but interpretations may often convey painful and unpalatable truths, which can provoke retaliation by the patient. Thus, the first impulse by the patient at an unconscious level is to deny and disavow any difficult, new formulation by the analyst, ablating it perhaps again and again before it can be accepted.

In the to and fro of the analytic engagement, there is struggle and negation that penetrates into both parties as each attempts to establish itself in the analytic dialogue. The mutual creation of the analyst and analysand, recognised in each moment of contact, is registered, ablated, then preserved symbolically, as *this* analyst and *this* analysand, who strive to allow no misunderstanding. The object is used in the unconscious, sometimes ruthlessly, in order to discover the self. The journey to the self is not always a peaceful one, particularly when the analyst's interpretations of psychoanalytic truth can taste like bitter medicine, and cannot always be combined with a spoonful of sugar. Interpretations can provoke; the patient can say no when yes is the truth, using denial, splitting, or disavowal. In the oscillation between the paranoid/ schizoid and the depressive positions, the patient's first response to interpretations may be to say, "No, that's not me; that sounds like criticism. I'm not that; I'm good. You are the one to blame." Analysis can feel like a battle to establish who's who and what's what, the self as distinct from other, and who one is in the analytic process. The negation of the other at the same time preserves, but this is nevertheless felt to be dangerous to the self, who may be frightened for his life, since his self *is* the other, the other that is destroyed *is* himself, and loss of the other is unthinkable. In our civilised world, much of the violence takes place in phantasy, conscious or unconscious, enviously attacking or destroying the other, affirming the self, negating the other.

For me, this situation inevitably brings to mind Winnicott's ideas in "The use of an object" (1969). Isn't this the same process described by Winnicott in which the object is destroyed? Aggressive attacks are made by the subject against the object, particularly at moments of separation or absence, and indeed continuously in order to be separate. The subject destroys the object; the patient obliterates the analyst in phantasy, particularly at the end of each session when he must gather and unify himself. But the analyst survives the destruction; he is there for the next session. For Winnicott, it is this survival that establishes the objectivity of the external world beyond the omnipotent control of the infant in the patient: aggressive phantasies are not so powerful; the reality of the other is not his to magically destroy. Explicit in Winnicott's notion is the next step: that the patient is then free to love and use the analyst, identifying with the surviving object (Abram, 2015), taking it into himself and recognising the other as one like himself.

Destroying the object appears elsewhere in the psychoanalytic literature: Perelberg (2015) wrote of the metaphorical killing of the father so as to create the social order, as did Freud in *Totem and Taboo* (1912–13). In the Oedipus myth, Oedipus kills his father and marries his mother, taking the place of the same-sex parent in the oedipal couple, which Freud theorised as a means, through identification, to acquire a feminine or masculine identity. Segal observed that the feeling state of the infant in relation to the breast-object was of destruction:

> On the depressive level, the feeling is that the introjected breast has been destroyed by the ego and can be re-created by the ego. (Segal, 1957, p. 395)

Klein wrote about the destruction of the object in the infant's struggle to internalise the good breast. Near the end of her life, in her paper "Some reflections on *The Oresteia*" (1963a), she intimated that matricide leads to individuation. Possibly misunderstood by her readers, her allusion to the death of the mother, illustrated by the Oresteia myth, must be understood, of course, as unconscious symbolic death. Orestes' murder of his mother, Klein notes, grants him freedom and independence at the cost of guilt, remorse, and depression, and ultimately a desire for reparation. Kristeva (2001) discusses Klein's notion of matricide in her *Oresteia* paper as essential to the establishment of the symbol, eventually enabling independence from the real mother and her body to give symbolic form to her functions, allowing mobile replacements and sublimations in place of the real nourishment of mother's breast. In Kristeva's account, she justifies what she takes as Klein's notion of matricide, saying that "… the symbol is the murderer of the mother" (Kristeva, 2001, p. 133). She says, why it is that we must finally do without her and move beyond her, "'I' know the sort of envy of which '

I' must rid myself—the overwhelmingly sadistic desire to work through, lose, and in a sense *kill*—so that I might acquire a baseline freedom to think" (p. 136, Kristeva's italics). Thus, in order to symbolise, to use symbols, the concrete maternal nurturing and feeding must be given up and transformed into mental activity. Could this be why Klein refused to answer her daughter Melitta Schmideberg's attacks in the Controversial Discussions, which allowed her to reject her mother, killing her off in order to think for herself, to go her own way and sever links with the analytic world? In any case, the persistence of the internal presence of the dysfunctional, persecutory, or bad mother must be killed, or modified and transformed, which may be the same thing. Furthermore, if the (m)other of infancy is not destroyed in unconscious phantasy, she remains alive as an omnipotent internal object, controlling and infantilising the subject.

In discussing the role of mourning for a dead object, Steiner (1993) wrote about the difficulty in recovering parts of the self if death is denied and mourning is obstructed: "… if he is unable to mourn, the projective identification becomes irreversible and the lost part of the self remains embedded in the object into which it has been projected" (p. 55). Steiner notes how difficult it is to relinquish the object upon whom one believes survival depends: "At this primitive level separation is indistinguishable from death" (p. 63).

Hegel described what happens when the destruction of the object is incomplete, when there is too much fear or guilt in the self to accomplish the negation, the death. The incomplete cancellation of the other self-consciousness leads to "dependent being" or the situation of lordship and bondage. The stronger master is able to ablate and negate, to become ascendant over the slave; the master exists for himself, the slave for the other. However, both slave and master need each other to an equal degree; the slave, afraid of risking death, identifies with the master's desire and works for him. But the master is also dependent on the slave because he needs him to maintain a relationship with the world through his labour. This era of struggle in the mind's development refers in Hegel to both individual development and to the history of slavery and the call for emancipation. When one self is subordinate to a stronger other, there is conflict and struggle that must be gone through, and an equality between them that is recognised eventually. When awareness of this situation dawns, when the other is seen as a self like him, this allows both slave and master to reach independence of being by recognising the other's existence as a human being like himself. Thus, the slave reaches self-existence, "being in himself" with a "mind of his own", recognised as such by the master (Hegel, 1964, p. 239).

Similarly, in the psychoanalytic view of growth and maturity, when, in the struggle around the work of internalising the good object, guilt and reparation for murderous unconscious phantasy are generated, then a new version of the (m)other is resurrected, who must then be killed again as separation and individuation take place. Eventually, there is an urge in the individual, with his good object inside, to find his own life and new sources of goodness, freeing himself from unequal relationships and finding a self that is liberated from subservience to parents, teachers, all others and the analyst as well. At this point, the person has, over time, developed a sense of identity and independence. As the analysis proceeds and develops, the psychic and somatic dependence on the analyst is transformed, the self and the other become separate and distinct, transferences and projections diminish, introjections increase, separations can be borne, and the analyst is seen as an indispensable separate other. Then each self exists as self, and the work of thinking together, taking turns, can proceed further. As in Hegel's phenomenology, once this stage of self-identity is established, there is a return to the beginning, a cyclical pattern without ending, a journey in which others continue to be necessary for realisation of the self. There is no end to the internal thrust of spirit that yearns for self-completion, that is, until life ends.

It must be said that projective identification is not always overtly violent, as indicated above; some explorations of identity can be more peaceable than this, the battle hidden under the surface. I will give examples of both kinds in this chapter. Presently, I wish to illustrate the aggressive projections that can take place in the struggle to find identity, the dialectic at work.

Terri

Terri was a beautiful young woman in her mid-twenties, training in a field of scientific research, who began analysis with great trepidation and fear, while at the same time knowing she needed to understand herself and her compulsive tendency to control situations and other people. Always independent, she spoke in a self-congratulatory way about her self-sufficiency, which she idealised. At the same time, she yearned for a relationship with a man and felt that something had to be done about what she knew was a dysfunctional way of relating that she couldn't understand. Up to the point of entering analysis she had managed to create her relationships in such a way that she revealed nothing of herself, controlling the other by pleasing and appeasing, asking questions and listening. Getting men to fall in love with her was not difficult, but when they did, displaying their need and desire for her, she would end the relationship, despising their neediness for her, for love and affection, as a sign of weakness, and reinstating her detached independence.

Initially refusing the couch, Terri found that while sitting in the chair she could speak to me, talking about herself, albeit with difficulty, and she found it interesting. After several months she began to trust me and the method a bit more, and she began to lie on the couch.

The sessions began to free Terri up and she said that friends had commented on how much more open she was with them. She spoke to me about her life, her friends, a man she liked, and told me things she had never told anyone before. She brought dreams that touched significant anxieties. It appeared that in spite of her ambivalence, the analysis might take off. However, her increasing revelations apparently alarmed her so much that she suddenly went away on a trip to visit her family who lived abroad, only informing me at the last minute. Having been sent away from home to a small convent boarding school in England from the ages of seven to eighteen by a mother who didn't actually like her, and told her this repeatedly, Terri nevertheless idealised her family, stoically tolerated with amusement her rejecting mother, overtly adored her father and two sisters, her aunts and cousins. When she returned from her trip she said she was surprised about the visit to her family home. She said that she always thought these trips would be wonderful before she went but in reality it had not been that wonderful; she'd had big arguments with her sisters and mother, and found her cousins loud and intrusive. She thought it would be like her childhood when long summers at home were wonderful. She told me that she felt guilty about how her life had changed due to her good education and good job, and how different to members of her family she had become. She told me that during the visit to her family she had had a terrible dream about her mother that had shocked and frightened her.

In the dream, she was in her grandmother's house with her mother, who had very long hair like her own (which her mother had never had in real life). Her mother was on a slab, in labour with twins, and there were many people running around, packing and preparing to leave. She was trying to comfort her mother, rubbing her back and looking after her, while wanting desperately to get away. Her mother needed a C-section. Terri could see that her mother's guts were falling out, her stomach open and bleeding. Her mother stood up and walked around with a white sheet wrapped round her, smeared and dripping with blood. Terri's associations were of a termination she herself had undergone that had resulted in dangerous complications. She went through the termination alone, not telling her mother and sisters because, she said, she would have had to comfort them instead of being comforted by them. The dream had a psychotic atmosphere. Terri's projections communicated her terror of exploring and revealing herself in analysis, as if her insides would concretely fall out. I could feel her horror of motherhood, as if birth were an appallingly dangerous event that had to be experienced alone; the twins, perhaps, stood for an identification of herself with her mother, having the same long hair, a needy, damaged mother whom she felt she must look after. Her terror was of being left alone, in need, with no one to care for her, but at the same time she despised this need. As I spoke to her of some of the meaning of the dream in terms of her anxiety, she listened carefully but became unsettled.

After this dream, instead of returning to the couch, she began to sit up in sessions or to miss them altogether, attributing this to her busy timetable in her field of scientific research. Then she came on time to a session and lay down. She told me a dream she'd had the night before about coming to a session and being in the consulting room with me. In the dream I was being sympathetic and understanding towards her and then tried to give her a hug. Forcefully, she said, "Ugh ... awful," referring with disgust to the kindly attitude and my attempt to hug her in the dream. The dream contained her desire for me to understand her and care for her, to which she reacted with disgust, showing how difficult it was for her to feel she needed anyone. This was a prime illustration, to my mind, of the dialectic at work, the splitting-off and projection of her feelings of need and longing for closeness and affection, projecting them into me, denying and repudiating the need in herself. She felt it was unbearably weak to feel any need for another, revolting and awful. At that moment, I was made to feel I was the needy and rejected one, as she projected the disgusting need into me, and rejected me. In an attempt to return the projection to her, based on the dream she had told me and the previous knowledge I had of her fleeing from intimacy with men, I responded, "It seems that you want kindness and affection but when you can have it, it disgusts you and you dance out of reach." She replied to me with heavy sarcasm, "Ooh, can I write that down?" mocking me and again rejecting me, in the struggle to identify who was needy, as she insisted it was not her. I tried another tack, turning things into their opposite, and said, "I think you are afraid I will get to know you and be disappointed or rejecting." "Yes," she said, and I went on to link this with her relationship with her rejecting mother. The analysis was touch-and-go for a time, and I could see in her a struggle with the impulse to flee, to leave me with the projections of the painful need for love she had felt as a child and now, hoping to get rid of it. I was to feel the abandonment she had experienced from her mother, not her, as she refused to acknowledge that what she felt was an alien projection of the need to be close.

In the exploration of Terri's internal world, there was a terrible fear of contact with a malign maternal object and her denied hatred and rage towards her mother, as well as a good maternal object that she feared would enslave or weaken her. It appeared that in the first months of analysis she perceived me and the analytic process as new and helpful, but after her visit to her family, getting more in touch with their reality and her deprivation and her need for closeness with me, she negated and disowned these emotions, becoming wary of the possibility of contact with a frightening internal world. Sadly, before we could go further, her training required her to work in another town some distance from London and analysis had to end.

Otherness

In examining the psychoanalytic literature, otherness appears most often in connection with difference, the analytic work over time of establishing self and other as separate and different. British analysts work diligently on this issue, proceeding as if the analysis of separation and separateness is sufficient to enable the individual to find self-identity and to relate to a separate, real other. In regard to this important issue, separateness is necessary but not sufficient to enable the self to be experienced in relation to the otherness of objects. One of the few analysts who have addressed this question is Spillius:

> ... one of the essential aspects of the depressive position is the individual's increasingly realistic perception of the "otherness" and "separateness" of his objects, together with recognition of his own identity as separate from but related to his objects. (2007, p. 201)

André Green (2000) wrote of "the otherness of the other". By this I believe he meant that although the other can be known as other, there is always an aspect that remains unknown and that must be respected as such. Green wrote:

> ... self-definition and respect for otherness can be regarded equally as the goals of analysis. It is commonly agreed, at least in my analytic community, that the discovery of otherness should be the aim of analysis, not only in the transference relationship, but also in what we can grasp of the relationship of the analysand with others, especially with intimates. We can claim even that all of the analytic work tends to this result. This is true also of the personal analysis of the analyst. (2000, p. 157)

However, there remains the intriguing question of what it means to encounter the analyst as other and whether it is possible for the other to be perceived without projections. To take up a point of contention, Birksted-Breen and Flanders (Birksted-Breen et al., 2010, p. 31) have pointed out that the French believe that the British have no concept of "otherness": that self and other consist of and are solely constructed by projective and introjective identification. If this is so, a sense of "otherness" as a phenomenon, the recognition and appreciation of the other as external, not us, may be eluded in analysis.

The question of otherness has not been fully addressed in British analysis, yet there is the assumption that the analyst as external other is required not only to contain and reflect the patient but also to bring definition, substance, and truth to the analytic enquiry through interpretation. Therefore, the encounter with otherness would need to include contact between the analyst's and patient's personality, beyond the interpretation of projections. However, there is some truth in the notion that there is a commonly held belief in the British psychoanalytic culture that objects are without external reality but made up solely of projections. This view, to me, overlooks the quality of the emotional contact between the two, whether it is tenderness and intimacy or emotional clashes, there are the sense impressions, emotional currents, and ideation that signal the presence of two separate sentient beings. Klein believed that contact with the other as such is possible later in the analysis after the outcome of the battle, in the depressive position, when each participant has a sense of identity and the other can be accepted as he is, when projections diminish, when there is no more idealisation or denigration, when the intensity of oedipal love abates and the oedipal object is relinquished, and the other is experienced as needed and loved. Empathy is necessary, sensitively tuning into the other to see him as he is, to discern self from other, at times returning projections that are "not me", exploring differences. The analyst as an individual real object, both similar and different from the self, is hard won through the dialectical analytic process. Bion's formulation of this would be to say that when the fury that we can't control or possess the love object becomes less, when love and hate diminish in intensity, curiosity, K, and the wish to know the other take precedence. Essentially, in spite of ourselves, most of us want to know and understand the world of others outside the self. That is, unless narcissism triumphs.

There is, however, something mysterious in the notion of "otherness", carrying with it, as it does, a sense of awe or trepidation, as if referring to an "absolute other" such as the gods, death, or otherworldly ghosts, or some other unknown dimension that is not a part of us. We look for ourselves in the other and are uneasy when we can't find it, when there is an appearance of otherness we can't comprehend; we have a tendency to try and tame otherness, to make it our own. In our possessive wish to construe our objects as known and belonging to us, to create familiarity, perhaps to dispel anxiety or to enhance our narcissism, we have a tendency to think of things as "ours"—our partner, our friend, our neighbour, our country, our planet—in an unending expansion and extension of ourselves (Roth, 2003). What about the unknown aspects of our objects that we haven't yet seen, their depths, the unfathomable otherness of them? To assume we know, to relate to appearances, to what we think we know of the other, or to put them in a category, is incomplete and in error. How wrong we can be if we pigeonhole people; there is always more: unseen aspects, depths, changes, developments. Respect for the other as other, as not fully known, is the beginning of empathy.

Upon entering psychoanalysis, the encounter with the analyst represents a step into the unknown. De M'Uzan (2010) takes up the encounter with otherness in a discussion of Freud's paper "The 'Uncanny'" (1919h), in which Freud describes experiences of fright upon meeting the unfamiliar and unknown. For me, de M'Uzan is suggesting in his paper that the ambiguous situation of meeting the otherness of the analyst is at first felt as bizarre, disturbing, and fascinating, an uncanny experience of strangeness, of ambiguity, in which there is uncertainty, where distinctions are erased and boundaries are blurred, the boundaries between "inside and outside, ego and non-ego, the subject and the object, the familiar and the alien". De M'Uzan writes that this experience throws up "the indeterminate nature of identity" (de M'Uzan, 2010, p. 206). These moments of strangeness stimulate projective identifications, opening up new pathways to self and otherness, disturbing the existing self-organisation and creating a disequilibrium that frees up the bound-together parts of the ego that are rigid and fixed. This ambiguity, he emphasises, is an essential activity of the mind, expanding identity, giving access to parts of the personality as yet unconscious or unborn.

Lack of the other and otherness

In this brief clinical vignette, I will describe the dilemma of a patient who, without a sense of an other outside himself, of an object that could contain him, recognise him, and reflect back who he was, had constructed a solipsistic world of narcissistic self-containment. His fear of emotional contact entailed a terror of falling into space and losing himself.

Mr B was a man of fifty who began analysis because of depression. He was intelligent and successful in his career, working in a high-pressure field, and living a manic social life on the weekends, fuelled by alcohol and drugs. Not long into the analysis it could be clearly seen why, for him, any dependency on others was dangerous: the other did not exist and it would be tantamount to projecting himself into outer space were he to put an emotional investment into relationships. In the sessions, I felt I had no existence for him. He projected nothing, spoke as if to himself, and proceeded to explore his life in an intellectual abstract way. Whatever containment his mother had to offer, and it did appear she was unemotional and out of touch, he had freed himself from dependence on her early on. He couldn't remember ever wanting to tell her anything or finding anything at home that interested him as he was growing up. He spent as much time as possible away from home, at his school or participating in sports. Rejecting any dependency or need of the (m)other, he had constructed self-containment and self-sufficiency very early in his life, turning inwards towards himself and his own gratifications and pleasures.

However, Mr B had become depressed due to significant losses in his life and sought analytic treatment. As a child, one huge crack had appeared in his "fortress of I", and I felt this was the precipitating factor in his defensive narcissism. When he was twelve years old, a girl of ten was brought to visit the family and he spent the day and evening with her, talking and playing. During the evening, the girl told him she wanted to kiss him and she did, which set off an emotional explosion in Mr B; he was flooded with powerful excitement and strange, over-whelming, and terrifying emotions. There was a feeling of horror in the consulting room as he described the experience, as if all his inner light, energy, and love poured out of him into a whirling, infinite universe, traumatising and horrifying him. In the room with him, I felt projected into me the terror and panic of seeing all love and inner contents stream-ing away, uncontained and lost. The loss was complete when the girl left the next day and he never saw her again. He attributed the origins of his depression and accompanying panic to this event, which he had never told anyone about. Not having had, or refusing, containment from his mother as a boy, he had no experience or expectation of a container that could supply him with anything he needed. The kiss had triggered off a massive experience of the lack of a containing object and a gigantic sense of loss that confirmed to him that he could not depend on anyone outside himself. It was apparent to me that his whole life was organised around never again having to experience this trauma.

After he had recounted to me the powerful experience with the girl together with the attendant emotional projections,—this imago appeared repeatedly in various forms in the analytic dialogue, linking to various moments of his life, his losses, and his depression. I believed Mr B felt contained and I began to exist as an other person. The trauma of the kiss was probably a screen memory of the loss of his mother's breast, and it was up to the containment and kiss of psychoanalysis to repair him.

However, in my encounter with him and attempts to understand him and reflect his identity as I saw it, there was struggle and negation in the dialectic. He would repudiate my remarks with, "I have no wish to be close to you; I dislike intimacy," or, "I can remember nothing about my early childhood with my mother. She was unimportant, insignificant, she has nothing to do with me now," or, "You speak about the break as if I should care that you are going away." He would go on the offensive, saying aggressively, "I have come here and worked hard to the best of my ability, trying to tell you about myself. Nothing has changed; I'm going in circles. When am I going to get better?" In the infrequent sessions in which he would be overtly angry with me I felt I had become real and present, a container for his projections. In the to and fro of the analysis, he expected me to do his thinking for him, remembering nothing of our work between sessions, not only magically expecting me to change him—the kiss in reverse—but projecting his thinking apparatus into me to think for him, then denying and negating my interpretations. But as time went on, he began to be more thoughtful, recognising and reclaiming lost parts of himself, including his need for others.

The good and the bad object

The next brief vignette illustrates the situation in the analytic dialectic in which the good and bad parts of the parents were split, the good parts repressed and the bad parts projected into the analyst. Ella was a young woman in her early twenties, lost in an extended adolescence and without a sense of who she was or what she wanted. She had hated her father for many years, which left her with a fear of closeness to men and without any belief that she could form a good libidinal relationship. Her parents had divorced when she was a baby and she felt sorely cheated in not having grown up with the presence of a helpful father. She had internalised a voice that told her nothing she did was any good, linked, I believed, with what she felt was rejection by her father, and she would say to me repeatedly, "How could I be worth anything having a dad who didn't want to know me and a mother who didn't treat me as special and was always trying to tell me what to do. It has left me with no self-belief."

In our encounter, she mistrusted and was suspicious of me in the transference, as she believed I was trying to get her to conform to her mother's values and wishes, forcing upon her the requirements of society, to take responsibility for herself, find a career, complete a master's degree and get a good job. She felt sure I disapproved of her late nights out drinking with friends and she rejected my interpretations as attempts to manipulate her to conform. She felt certain that I was a representative of a middle-class society she was reluctant to join and there was a battle around her projections into me of disapproval of her activities, her conviction that I wanted her, just as her mother did, to make her conform to a boring, conventional life. For a long time I was the recipient of projective identifications of what she believed to be a demanding, argumentative, disapproving mother, as she complained vociferously about both mother and me. It took many interpretations of her belief about me, regularly negated and flung back at me, before Ella could contemplate the possibility that I wasn't judging or trying to manipulate her.

There were terrible rows with her mother and one of the things she most hated about her childhood and adolescence was that her mother frequently sent her, against her will, to visit her father who was living abroad, which felt to her like a punishment. According to her reports, he was never glad to see her, would ignore her or bully her, or leave her to the care of his new wife. Ella hated him; he had let her down as a father and there wasn't anything good she could say about him. Even after he died she still reviled him. Inevitably, I became a recipient of negative father projections—for I was also the father she felt forced to visit—as she told me repeatedly that it was a pain in the backside to come to sessions.

After having spoken at length over the course of many sessions about her father's many failures, my patient had a dream about him which was the first happy feeling about him that she could remember. In the dream she met her father in a shopping mall and he had brought with him a little dog for her, which she loved. She had the feeling of being taken to a fair, a special event just for her. He spoke to her with sympathy and understanding; there was a good feeling between them, and they hugged each other with happiness. She cried all through the session as she spoke of the dream. It felt to her like an apology from him, the appearance of good feelings and memories, as if he had redeemed himself, an extension of the last conversation they had had at his bedside before he died. I felt it was the working-through of anger towards the bad father that had brought forth the split-off good father, much loved in early childhood. While my patient was working through the dialectical good and bad aspects of her father, she was also working through the good and bad aspects of the analyst, and I could be seen, more realistically, as someone she perceived was on her side and helpful. She also began to get along better with her mother. As her projective identifications of bad aspects of the object into me as analyst were interpreted, and the interpretations negated over and over by the patient, then eventually accepted, they allowed the good and bad object to come together in in my patient's mind. The defensive split that protected her from the pain of loss of her father was dismantled; the patient experienced sadness for the loss of a father viewed more realistically, and whom she had barely got to know.

* * *

In the establishment of a central identity, as discussed in Chapter One, object relations compose our internal world and are essential to our external world and who we are. We need the other, both internally and externally, to remind us who we are and to contain us. In the case of the narcissist, the other is missing, excluded; being self-defined, the narcissist does not see himself accurately, although he believes that he does. In love with his self-image in the pool, lacking the other's "recognition", contact, and mirroring, his true identity is obscured. When the narcissist subsumes the goodness of the other and otherness into himself, he positions himself in the centre of the universe; he is all. Instead of a planet circling round the sun, he believes he is the sun. The dilemma of narcissism will be addressed in the next three chapters.

CHAPTER THREE

Narcissism and unconscious phantasy

To love oneself is the beginning of a lifelong romance.

—Oscar Wilde, 1894

I am the only person in the world I should like to know thoroughly.

—*Lady Windermere's Fan*, Oscar Wilde, 1891

These quotes illustrate in a nutshell the popular view of narcissism as a love relationship and preoccupation with the self, originally portrayed by the myth of Narcissus who fell in love with his own reflection. Foremost in relationship difficulties between the self and the other we find the culprit narcissism and its accomplice, lack of empathy. Standing in the way between the self and good human relationships is often an overvalued identity and inflated sense of self.

In psychoanalysis, the notion of narcissism grew from being seen as simple self-love into a much more complex phenomenon posing wide-ranging problems in the personality and existing somewhere between neurotic and psychotic states. Within the psychoanalytic literature, narcissism is described in several ways: as ordinary healthy narcissism or as the narcissistic disorders of the personality that present clinically, which may be defensive, libidinal, or destructive. First, as seen in ordinary life, when love or life is disappointing or turns bad there can be a turning away from love objects or the external world for a time towards self-love, for the restoration of self-esteem. This is everyday, even healthy, narcissism, to which it is important to have recourse in some degree in order to recover from life's slings and arrows, from the invasion of too much otherness, and as general internal encouragement. However, when there is too much dependence on self-love or when narcissistic formations are installed in early life due to a failure in the mother–infant experience, libidinal narcissism can become a fixed structure of the personality, an identity characterised by self-importance.

Then, there are the defensive narcissistic disorders, the pathological personality structures in which a fortification or psychic retreat (Steiner, 1993) has been formed by the ego to protect and defend a highly vulnerable inner self. Withdrawal to this retreat is meant to protect, but actually deforms the ego in its intended function, which is to mediate between the inner and outer worlds. When the ego and its defences are overly valued and highly cathected, contact with internal and external reality is compromised. There is distortion of external reality by projective identification of undesirable parts of the self and of internal reality by introjection of only the good self-image.

In what has been termed destructive narcissism, following Rosenfeld (1971, 1987), there is a force in the personality that is hostile to object relations and rejects the non-self, an aggressive configuration in which there is idealisation of the omnipotent destructive parts of the self (Rosenfeld, 1971, 1985) and rejection of otherness. The different kinds of narcissistic states can be fluid and changeable, existing together, forming and re-forming in a fluid network according to presiding experience, as part of the neurotic personality. On the other hand, libidinal, defensive, or destructive narcissism can be pathological, stable, and fixed; they can be highly organised to keep others out.

In this chapter I will not discuss ordinary narcissism but focus on the latter types—libidinal, defensive, and destructive narcissism—and will show how they are created to protect and repair the vulnerable self from inner and outer threats, forming a defensive organisation or psychic retreat. Steiner points out that the complex matrix of the psychic retreat is not so much a place of calm but an uneasy attempt to keep unconscious anxiety at bay. He writes: "… defensive organisations serve to bind, to neutralize, and to control primitive destructiveness, whatever its source" (Steiner, 1993, p. 4). In my view, at the heart of narcissistic organisations are terrifying phantasies that are kept unconscious within the defensive organisation, and are concerned with the safety of the self from attack by inner persecutory objects. I maintain that it is important in the treatment of narcissistic disorders to locate and to interpret the unconscious phantasy together with narcissistic wounds and other defensive issues, recognising that buried in the unconscious is terror of aggression, destructiveness, abandonment, and loss.

First of all, I would like to present the following brief vignette that poses the question: is this an example of Rosenfeld's destructive narcissism together with psychotic anxiety existing in the depths of a narcissistic personality? Or is this an example of a narcissistic structure that is primarily defensive in nature, a defensive retreat involving hostility and aggression but primarily designed to preserve the self? This material was not a dream or a fantasy per se, but material that inferred psychic structures in a difficult patient, in the form of an account of a film told to her therapist which, when discussed as aspects of the patient's inner world, was valuable in unlocking defences and promoting understanding. This was a case I supervised in the NHS, a young woman whose work life and relationships were very disturbed; she had resigned from a series of jobs after rowing with managers, indignant that she should be asked to do anything she didn't want to do, and she left potential partners believing them all to be inferior. Her therapist found her difficult to engage, hostile, and aggressive; for example, the patient claimed after a few sessions that she didn't need therapy, often didn't show up for sessions, and left the therapist feeling useless, attacked, and rejected. After some months of the therapist's frustrated attempts to reach the patient, she came into a session and exclaimed, "I saw the best film I've ever seen last night, it was called *The Divide*." As she described it in great detail, it was apparent that the film resonated strongly with her and it revealed to the therapist for the first time something about the patient's profound unconscious anxieties. In the film there was a nuclear explosion that entirely destroyed New York City. A group of people went into an underground bunker to escape the devastation, but something strange and alien tried to enter through the door. The people barricaded the door. Then they all went mad inside the bunker. There was rape and killing; the good people turned bad and the bad ones, strangely, were portrayed as more interesting. The patient, who had been sexually abused by her stepfather for a number of years, could recognise when the link was made by her therapist that the film represented an image of her internal world, with no good object inside, and with her explosive rage directed towards the outside world, as she shut people out and hid away. Her anger about the sexual abuse and her lack of protection as a child was so great that it felt as if it would annihilate her objects, so she had formed a defensive organisation. This meant she shut out her therapist as an alien and sealed the door, but then felt she was in danger of going mad. Letting in the therapist to form a libidinal relationship was forbidden by the mad gang inside the barricade. Although the film narrative could not be considered an exact map of the patient's internal world, it gave a view and words to approximately describe unconscious forces that had not been previously accessible.

In supervision I urged the therapist to interpret the patient's explosive rage—which she believed was hugely destructive and dangerous—to show her how the patient tried to get rid of it by projecting it outside. I explained to the therapist that when she knocked on the door of the patient's mind to be let in, speaking to her in a session, "although she wants to let you in, she fears you are alien and toxic, full of her projected rage, and she blocks the door. But shutting herself off from you leaves her in a bunker in the hands of a violent mad gang; internally, she is shut up with murderous parts of herself, a violent psychotic part and a destructive primal scene." As the supervisee took up the patient's hostility in the transference, commenting on her murderous rage and her fear of retaliation, and how she hid herself away in a bunker, the patient began to attend sessions more regularly and to be more present. There was more contact with the part of her that wanted help, which grew over time to form a positive transference to the therapist as a good object.

The film, of course, cannot be equated with the patient's actual psychic structures, but it hinted at avenues of enquiry that turned out to be fruitful. Neither the film images nor the patient exhibited triumph in destructiveness; however, within the bunker there were excited descriptions of murderousness, sadism, masochism, eroticism, and fascination with bad characters that appeared to arise from her child sexual abuse, a scenario that was an admixture of defensive and destructive elements in a narcissistic retreat.

* * *

Rosenfeld has been a major contributor to the understanding of pathological narcissism, and his distinction between libidinal and destructive narcissism was pivotal: ever since he described these two basic forms of narcissism, this distinction has been taken up widely by the psychoanalytic community in Britain (Rosenfeld, 1985). Rosenfeld characterised libidinal narcissism by the belief in the special value of the self and the diminution of the other:

> In considering narcissism from the libidinal aspect one can see that the overvaluation of the self plays a central role, based mainly on the idealization of the self. Self-idealization is maintained by unconscious, omnipotent introjective and projective identifications with good objects and their qualities. In this way the narcissist feels that everything that is valuable relating to external objects and the outside world is part of him, or is omnipotently controlled by him. (Rosenfeld, 1985, p. xx)

This formulation follows the model of Freud's "purified pleasure ego", a primitive state in which the infant experiences goodness and pleasure as identical with his ego, projecting pain and un-pleasure outside.

Regarding destructive narcissism, Rosenfeld described a primary hostility to relationships, idealising destructiveness:

> Similarly, when considering narcissism from the destructive aspect, we find that again self-idealization plays a central role, but now it is the idealization of the omnipotent destructive parts of the self. They are directed both against any positive libidinal object relationship and any libidinal part of the self which experiences need for an object and the desire to depend on it. (Rosenfeld, 1971, p. 173)

Rosenfeld described the destructive narcissistic organisation in the internal world as functioning like a mafia gang, stepping in to hijack the patient and prevent the formation of libidinal relationships. Both he and Freud believed that destructive narcissism is a manifestation of the death instinct: a narcissistic pleasure in destructiveness for its own sake. For Lena, the omnipotent patient I describe at length in the next chapter, the analysis went through periods in which destructive narcissism and the death instinct could be seen to hold sway. However, in this chapter I will discuss libidinal narcissism and describe two such patients, highlighting the role of the superego and unconscious phantasy in narcissism.

The narcissist and the other

The undue cathexis of the self in narcissistic disorders means that the person's capacity to empathise with the other, that is, their ability to see things from the other's point of view, entering into the other's experience, and feeling and understanding something of the internal world of the other, is hindered. The narcissist has difficulty in terms of ordinary human interdependence with the other, cherishing independence and self-sufficiency, feeling diminished by need for the external object; in valuing and needing another his sense of his own power and omnipotence is threatened and his envy and aggression are triggered. Segal took up the view that it is the aggressive aspects of narcissism that predominate; she stated that narcissism and envy are "two sides of the same coin" (Segal, 2007, p. 225) and that there was no need to distinguish between them. Klein differed substantially from this view. Self-love could redeem, she thought, as long as relationships with the other could also be sustained. She proposed that self-love serves as a defence against envy; that is, if one can love the self, one need not suffer so painfully "the green-eyed monster" (Klein, 1957, p. 181–182). She emphasised that narcissism coexists with object relations and consists of periodic withdrawal to the internalised good object (Klein, 1952, p. 51).

There is a particular form of narcissism in which self-hate is rampant instead of love, where there is a preoccupation with the badness of one's character and omnipotent self-blame, as was the case for a young woman patient of mine who claimed to be a failure at everything, responsible for all the misfortunes in her family, worthless and unlovable in every way. The primitive destructiveness of her superego had paralysed her personality. It posed a threat to her self and her survival in that, until she started analysis, her strategy was to meekly placate the superego, expecting nothing in life, succumbing to guilt, admitting badness, living carelessly and at times dangerously, in a constant state of *mea culpa*.

The severe superego plays an important role in narcissism, functioning as an internal object made up of a law-giver and conscience but suffused with projected aggression from the subject. Bion, writing of the early environment and the need for the infant to be loved and to introject loving parents as good objects, said that the outcome of a failure of maternal love and containment "is an object which, when installed in the patient, exercises the function of a severe and ego-destructive superego" (Bion, 1959, p. 107). When an envious, destructive superego is formed within the personality, the ego may attempt to achieve a state of narcissistic perfection by conforming to the ideal ego in order to appease the superego. But this effort is doomed to be unsuccessful not only because of the impossibility of reaching perfection but because, as the ego attains greater levels of goodness, the envious superego mounts ever more destructive attacks against the ego, disabling its functioning. Britton (2003, p. 120) made the point that the ego's solution is found by forming a defensive narcissistic organisation in which a collusive relationship is created between the self and an idealised version of the self. In this pact there is an identification of the self with the ideal ego, which has the function of cancelling out the ego's need for love from the superego.

Hinshelwood (2009) has argued that Klein was working the whole time in the area of narcissism, although she didn't say this explicitly; that is, she was working in the area of defending or repairing the self from the ravages of damage through projective identification, the fragmentation and loss of projected good and bad parts of the self. Ultimately, in Hinshelwood's view, Klein's work of analysing the oscillation between paranoid/schizoid and depressive states is actually the battle with narcissistic processes and threats to the ego as the patient attempts to deny unwelcome interpretations that could bring about paranoid states or depressive anxiety.

Following Bion's formulation that "… the non-psychotic personality was concerned with … a conflict of ideas and emotions … the psychotic personality was concerned with the problem of repair of the ego" (Bion, 1957, p. 57), Hinshelwood proposed that:

> This concern with the psychotic-like "repair of the ego" connects with the notion of a narcissistic wound which must be protected and becomes a central feature of a person's endeavour in life. Klein's emphasis on this "deeper layer of the unconscious" implies consistently working with a continuously active narcissistic level of the unconscious. The issue is not therefore that some personalities

are narcissistic, and others not; the state of affairs is that the narcissistic level in all personalities comes through more in some than in others. (Hinshelwood, 2009, p. 2)

It is familiar territory to think of the narcissist as harbouring a vulnerable emotional interior self that is susceptible to hurt from others. We all disguise our susceptibilities behind a persona that faces the world; however, pathological narcissistic structures are of a different order and involve an overvaluation of self that is organised in a complex, deep, and wide network of defences, complaints, and resentments. The narcissistic organisation is an attempt to shore up an injured ego by means of magical narcissistic repair, and to sideline the superego by the ego's alliance with the ideal ego, fostering a belief in an admirable, good self. It is designed to nurture, protect, and repair the ego's narcissistic wounds stemming from rejection, abandonment, or envy, and to defuse internal anxieties arising from persecutory objects and a destructive superego. Further to this, I suggest there is a psychotic phantasy buried in the narcissistic organisation, possibly fears of fragmentation, annihilation, depletion, or aggressive explosions that complicate the defence. So it was with the two patients I will discuss below.

Mr A

Mr A, aged forty-three, sought analysis since he had been suffering from irritability and ennui for some time and was bored with his job and his marriage. He and his wife had not had children. Mr A grew up as an only child with a father who disciplined him harshly, and he was sent to a strict boarding school; his mother was depressive, and was represented as a vague, shadowy figure. In the first session Mr A told me he didn't know what was wrong. "There must be more to life than this," he said. He had always thought he had a special destiny that would eventually be revealed to him, but this had not happened. He settled into four sessions per week and into free association, taking to the analytic setting, speaking fluently about his life and his difficulties, his parents and various relationships, appearing to be getting on with it. His associations were articulate and full of metaphors and insights. However, he left little space for me and I felt a sense of redundancy, wondering what on earth I would be able to give him. Reflecting on this countertransference, I could see that I was meant to feel admiration for him and his performance, just as he admired himself as a libidinal object.

As time went on there were signs of profound restlessness and a deep unhappiness that he could not name, but these were difficult to contact; he kept his innermost feelings at a distance. When I tried to reach him, basing my comments on the emotional hints or signifiers I could feel in the room, he paid little attention and slipped away. The pattern in his responses to my comments and interpretations showed a lack of interest in what I had to say. Mr A would politely stop speaking while I was talking, then resume speaking where he'd left off, clearly not listening to me or taking anything in. Alternatively, in response to my interpretations, he would answer, "Yes, but ...", or, "No ...", or, "Yes, I know that ...", brushing off my words, then going on with what he was saying. There was no resonance or associative response that allowed our two minds to meet. I offered interpretations around how difficult he found it to link up with my thoughts or feelings, and that he found it easier to carry on a dialogue with himself, that it was as if I wasn't in the room, but he tended to react to these with silence. I felt ignored; he felt impenetrable. These countertransference feelings communicated to me something of an early trauma I felt he had experienced in regard to a non-responding, impenetrable, depressed mother, and that he needed time for the ongoing work in the transference to touch him and for him to be able to construe the analytic situation as consisting of an object and a container that he could trust with his vulnerable self.

I settled down to study him further. I felt that, along with the defences he maintained so rigorously, he had constructed a self-sufficient, narcissistic organisation, a "fortress of I", but that he paid the price by living in a lonely, solipsistic world without emotional contact with others. I could feel the powerful resistance that Rosenfeld (2008, p. 112) described as stemming from a superior, omnipotent attitude. Mr A's good education and intelligence meant that he looked down on his less well-educated wife, his parents, and the person he believed I was in the transference, which I did not allow to go uninterpreted. Within his inflated self-image it transpired that he not only believed he "knew it all", but he believed he could predict what would happen in the future, feeling certain of the outcome. And he knew best how things should be done, instructing family members and friends on what they should be doing. This included the analysis, about which he instructed me in detail. He had a curious attitude to time, which he felt would bend to his wishes, along with other aspects of reality, making things into what he wanted them to be. I recognised all these characteristics as typical of the clinical presentation of the narcissistic personality.

For some time, I spoke to him about his lack of trust in me, the distance he kept between us, how hard it was for him to let me in, his determination to be self-sufficient and not need anyone, which slowly brought us a bit closer. Then, I could make more frank interpretations about his sense of superiority and entitlement, his knowing everything and knowing best, and how he often didn't listen to me and take in what I said. He responded angrily to these interpretations, yet there was a begrudging acknowledgement that they were true. At times he felt persecuted simply by my "otherness" and would hit out. Then, as his defensive organisation loosened, his dreams began to reveal terrifying scenarios: he dreamed repeatedly of being chased by two men who intended to kill him and he could find no place of safety. In other versions, he was taken to a place where he was to be executed by firing squads, axes, or guillotines, dreams that I consistently interpreted in the transference. In one particularly terrifying dream, a ferocious wolf appeared in a dark wood, which I interpreted as his rage towards me, feeling threatened that I would damage him. His rigid narcissistic defence made sense when seen in a threefold way: (1) to rectify and repair his wounded, fragile self that felt rejected by his mother and judged harshly by his father, (2) as a retreat from the non-responding impenetrable primal object that made him doubt the presence of dependable external objects, and (3) as a protection against murderous internal objects, forms of the malign superego, as revealed by his dreams. As his analytic mother, I worked to receive, contain, and transform his projections, and in the transference he gradually began to see me as less persecutory and more helpful.

Mr C

Mr C grew up without a father as the only child of a busy professional mother who was often absent. Left on his own much of the time as he was growing up, immersed in reading his books, alone with his vivid imagination and his anxieties, it seemed that a solipsistic inner world of imagination began then, with himself as the potent centre, created to stave off feelings of abandonment and loneliness and his need for closeness to others. As an adult, in spite of his strong personality, he was hugely insecure in his emotional life and unable to have an emotional or sexual relationship with a woman. In his professional life, although in possession of a prodigious intellectual gift, he had never reached his potential because of paranoid fears and anxieties around his own masculine sexuality, which had consequently hampered him in having potent interactions with the outside world. His unconscious oedipal castration anxiety was intense, as it emerged in the analysis, due to childhood phantasies that his father had been away in prison and would return to punish him for the longing and love he felt towards his mother. He had erected phallic narcissism as a compensatory defensive organisation, with a heightened cathexis of and pride in an ideal self.

In the beginning of his long four-times-weekly analysis, his associations revealed a racy, busy mind full of fantasies: rapid, fragmented, and often of a paranoid nature. He told me of a recurring image he had of Atlas holding up the world, which I understood as a derivative of an unconscious phantasy of himself as powerful and burdened with responsibilities for the world. Always having had his high intelligence commended, he told me that he had always believed he could do anything at all that he chose, take up any profession, master any skill. He fantasised that he was an anthropologist, rather contemptuously studying humans as an inferior herd to which he didn't belong. He was, by his own admission, "grandiloquent", looking down on others from a great height and feeling morally superior. In contrast with this, much of his spontaneous fantasy in the sessions was about finding a place to hide away, seeking safety from a dangerous world.

Without going into the details of his history, suffice it to say that when Mr C began analysis he was scarcely working, and it was evident that he lived in an omnipotent, narcissistic world of phantasy and magical thinking. Our early work was around achieving insight into this world and what it meant in terms of his ideas, fantasies, and plans: he held the belief that he did not have to make efforts to actually put his ideas into practice in the real world, to realise and actualise his thoughts and intentions. His unconscious magical thinking meant that he believed he had only to think something and it would happen automatically. Gradually, as I consistently interpreted this and he became aware of his difficulty in sticking with an idea and carrying it through to completion, his mind took on some capacity for order, both within and outside the sessions, and he began working on a project that turned into a very successful enterprise. Within the sessions his associations became less random and anxiety-laden, and more focused on thinking through his problems; nevertheless, given the considerable amount of psychotic anxiety in him, it was important to pay close attention to whatever was the main point of urgency from moment to moment in the sessions.

From the beginning he felt anxious about being in the room with me and at the same time felt that the sessions were a haven of safety and protection from a world in which he was under attack from his enemies. I consistently worked with his paranoid anxiety in relation to men in the outside world and particularly with his anxiety about being in the sessions with me. His fears gathered around the phantasy that I wanted to seduce him into an erotic relationship. (I discuss Mr C in greater detail in Chapter Seven on sexuality.) His fear that closeness to me would mean loss of control and result in a frightening erotic relationship, imagined as a primal scene phantasy of "the beast with two backs", a terrifying figure that appeared in his mind whenever he had thoughts of sex. He was also tormented by terrifying oedipal fantasies. Many times he would suddenly say, "I just had the fantasy that someone, an angry man, was about to come in through the door, very scary." I interpreted that he was afraid that my husband would enter the consulting room, feel angry seeing him there, and attack him for being close to me. I said that a jealous castrating father existed in his mind, furious that he had the attentions of his mother, and would somehow return to punish him. Mr C's narcissism was formed, from my perspective, to compensate for the helplessness he felt as a small boy in the face of abandonment and the terror of this central psychotic oedipal phantasy.

Consistent work in the transference on these phantasies modified Mr C's terrifying, primitive internal objects to a large degree. Initially experiencing me as a dangerous, frightening "other" saturated with his projections, he moved during this long analysis to a more benign view of me; although he continued to be wary and erected barriers between us, he spoke of the sense of protection, affection, and intimacy he felt being with me, and he was aware of me as a separate person with a life of my own about which he was curious. No longer did he omnipotently "create and destroy" me as part of himself, bringing me to life at the beginning of sessions and killing me off at the end (Winnicott, 1969), with no sense of continuity that we both existed in time.

Mr C became more in touch with both external and psychic reality, and the difference between them, establishing a less anxious, more stable identity; he could, to a degree, mourn his losses, but he began to complain that his life felt mundane. He felt unable to identify fully with the successful project he was directing in the external world, with his daily life with his partner, with the interesting social groups that he had contact with, or with his strong ethical and moral beliefs that gave him purpose. It was painful and puzzling for him to form a new a self-identity based on his real position in the world. Now that he no longer had the omnipotent belief that he could do anything he wanted, identifying with the powerful Atlas protector of the world, it was difficult to accept who he was. Would he go on doing what he was doing now for the rest of his life, he wondered, and not achieve the world-changing ambitions and creative works of genius that he had hoped for? The loss of the narcissistic sense of being very special meant coming to terms with a more ordinary existence in the real world, joining human society, with which he struggled as a painful and difficult achievement.

Discussion

Abraham (1919) has written of the way in which certain narcissists attempt to use the analysis for their narcissistic pleasure, resisting the analytic process in subtle ways and refusing to accept the analyst as a helpful, good object. These patients feel analysis to be an attack on their good self-image, which is avoided by taking control of the free association process, thus avoiding dependence and the positive transference, and all the while appearing to be freely associating. They tacitly identify with the analyst and attempt to analyse themselves.

My two patients were libidinal narcissists, not destructive narcissists in Rosenfeld's sense with a fundamental hostility towards objects, although at times they destroyed links with me or were attacking. Both patients attempted to defensively take control of the free-associative process in the way described by Abraham (1919). In each of them a narcissistic organisation involving an inflated self was formed to protect and repair a damaged self, so that letting me in threatened their identity, as if I would expose or diminish them, revealing a painfully inadequate, vulnerable inner self that they were afraid I would not be able to care for.

Speaking to patients about their overvalued selves is a tricky technical proposition, a matter of managing both defensive and aggressive aspects of the transference. Interpretations of narcissism can be painful and cause anger, disequilibrium, and fragmented states, until, if, and when, the interpretations can be metabolised. For example, when I spoke to Mr A about his dislike of taking in anything from me or of his sense of superiority and knowing best, he reacted with anger or with depressive anxiety, but soon bounced back to take control of the sessions. These interactions linked with his view of me as his critical, aggressive father and his angry rebellion that had been repressed but was reactivated in the transference.

In manic self-reparation, Mr C attempted to repair his wounded self by identifying with Atlas and an idealised vision of himself. As his grandiose self became eroded over time by the analytic process, he was not so pleased to find himself to be a human being like others, without super human powers. Both Mr A and Mr C had to mourn the loss of their ideal selves in the depressive position, involving self-acceptance and acceptance of me as an "other", a separate person. Gradually they both allowed a closer relationship with me, a trust that I was there for them.

As I have suggested, the failure of maternal containment and intense oedipal anxiety in my patients meant that an ego-destructive superego inhabited their internal world. When a mother is incapable of reverie and containment, or is absent for a significant period, the infant projects distress, inchoate beta elements, and receives back not alpha elements that could transform the distress into something meaningful, but an introject stripped of meaning, a destructive and aggressive superego object that attacks the ego. Both of my patients formed a narcissistic organisation not only to defend against threats from the outside, but to evade the superego's harshness in relation to a vulnerable self; self-love and identification with an ideal self were employed to avoid its demands and attacks. As Freud wrote in *Civilization and its Discontents*: "We are very often obliged, for therapeutic purposes, to oppose the super-ego, and we endeavour to lower its demands" (1930a, p. 143). Understanding and interpreting when the superego is actively attacking the self or turned against the analyst and his many faults and omissions helps to modify its impact. However, I believe there is a further aspect of dealing with narcissistic defences: the apprehension and interpretation of unconscious psychotic anxiety and its derivatives buried within the narcissistic matrix that threaten the safety of the self. I suggest it is labelled psychotic because of its unreality and its intensity. When analysis can come to grips with and transform these deep anxieties in regard to fears of destructiveness, annihilation, or death, together with an increased tolerance of object need and otherness, there can be more of a capacity for direct contact with both psychic reality and external reality, and most importantly, less fear in relating to others. Thus, in my view, analysis is not so much about finding a "true self" as shedding false concepts of self and gaining the capacity to relate to others in a genuine, less fearful way. Through the analytic method of analysing projective and introjective identification over time, there is the possibility of emerging from the narcissistic psychic retreat to meet the other in a shared space and real encounter. Like Prospero at the end of Shakespeare's *The Tempest*, who leaves his magical island, breaks his staff, drowns his book, and goes to Milan to be a regular person and do his job, he awakens from his dream world to enter the real world beyond his own ego.

In following the argument that analysing the psychotic anxiety embedded in the narcissistic matrix is crucial, I will present two patients in Chapter Five that illustrate this notion. In the next chapter I will focus on one patient, Lena, following her journey through a long analysis. Her main feature was omnipotence, but increasingly I came to view her as a destructive narcissistic who was harbouring a terror of her destructive potentiality.

CHAPTER FOUR

From omnipotence to ordinary potency and identity

Freud first discussed "omnipotence of thought" in *Totem and Taboo* (1912–13). It was a term taken from the analysis, in 1909, of the Rat Man, who believed that his thoughts would bring about the death of those he came into contact with. Freud believed that during childhood the individual passes through a stage of primitive, animistic thinking, leaving a residue that bears a "resemblance to the savages who believe they can alter the external world by mere thinking". He goes on to say about the belief in magic that, "Neurotics live in a world apart, where ... they are only affected by what is thought with intensity and pictured with emotion, whereas agreement with external reality is a matter of no importance" (1912–13, p. 86).

Since to some degree we are all neurotic, no one is entirely free from omnipotent thinking. Under conditions of frustration, obstruction, or helplessness, or great desire and desperation, all of us can slip into omnipotent magical thinking. But when substantial regions of the unconscious are taken over by omnipotent states, according to Freud, the stage is set for the development of both neurosis and psychosis. In the overt psychoses, omnipotent magical thinking is a familiar phenomenon in which delusions of being God, Satan, Hitler, or various other figures with fabulous powers to create or destroy, represent the extremes of a demolition of ordinary psychic reality and of normal mental functioning. Segal (1986) has underlined the importance of omnipotent states of mind in the aetiology of all mental disorders. As she put it: "In my view, all neurotic defences are rooted in psychotic omnipotence, particularly the omnipotent denial of psychic reality, that is, conflict, ambivalence, and the attendant depressive anxiety. These defences disturb both the growth of the ego and object relationships" (Segal, 1986, p. 216).

In this chapter I will describe the main features in the analysis of a patient with a narcissistic/borderline personality in which omnipotence, magical thinking, and manic defence were all significant features, used in attempts to establish dominance over the analytic relationship. An unconscious phantasy of omnipotent aggression, terrifying in its potential to destroy, was at the heart of this patient's defensive personality organisation, which, when it became conscious, enabled movement in the analysis.

Lena

The patient, Lena, was in mid-life when she began four-times-weekly analysis, which lasted for eight years. Lena's father committed suicide when she was two years old. Her mother remarried a year later, bringing into the household not only a stepfather but two step-sibs, and soon another child, a sister, was born. Lena told me her mother disliked physical contact with her children and was often brutal to her stepchildren. With five children in her charge, mother dealt with them by keeping them busy with household chores and firmly under her dictatorial control. She would threaten to leave the house, be taken to hospital, or commit suicide if they didn't obey her.

Lena's stepfather worked away from home during the week, returning at weekends. Bitter rows took place between the parents every Friday night, terrifying my patient, who was convinced that her stepfather would kill her mother, or vice versa, after having seen her mother once threaten her stepfather with a knife. Lena would lie awake at night, listening for hours to their angry voices, believing it was her constant vigilance that kept them from tearing each other to pieces.

In another example of obsessive magical thinking, when the nights were stormy and windy she was frightened that a large tree outside would fall onto the house killing her mother unless she stayed awake focusing intensely on the tree to ensure it did not fall. Instead of going outdoors to play, she would remain at her mother's side, wooden, rigidly self-contained, not speaking, never crying or allowing any emotion at all, to the fury of her mother. Lena's consolation consisted in reading magical fairy tales in which charming princes rescued maidens or Bluebeard murdered his wives. For this traumatised girl, omnipotence was an aid to surviving her childhood. Fairy tales, magical control of her violent, disturbed parents, and projections of her aggression defended her against a frightening world.

Successful at school, a graduate in English, and later performing well in her job as a corporate manager, she functioned by being masochistically compliant, "meek as a mouse", with her bosses and in her relationships with men. When she began analysis she had been living on her own for several years. She described to me how she spent weekends and evenings alone in her flat, tidying up, but mostly sitting quietly doing nothing, in a hazy, mindless state, waiting until Monday when she could go to work. Keeping her mind still, which she told me required effort, calmed and soothed her. I understood this to mean that were she to allow any freedom to her mind, unmodified primitive emotions, obsessively denied and projected (Klein, 1935), might overtake her.

Thus, she kept all stimuli at bay, inner and outer, a situation Abraham (1911) described in melancholic narcissists. He notes that only in seclusion can such patients allow themselves pleasure; they are disturbed by the intrusion into their space of "any living being or lively external impression", and so they withdraw into unconscious auto-erotism and narcissistic self-preoccupation, constructing a carefully controlled, stimulus-free world.

Abraham wrote of the similarity between severe cases of obsessional neurosis and some features of melancholic depression that aptly describe Lena's initial state and the early stages of treatment. He wrote that "… a hostile attitude towards the external world is so great that [their] capacity for love is reduced to a minimum" (1911, p. 139). Due to their projections of hate and murderous wishes for revenge, Abraham continued, these patients get the idea that others hate *them* because of their defects; they prefer to believe they are despised by others rather than see that they shun the world because of their own aggression. They suffer from unconscious guilt and depressive affect due to their belief that they omnipotently kill or injure others by means of their thoughts, punishing themselves by the adoption of masochistic tendencies, through which they gain pleasure from suffering. All this was evident in my patient, Lena.

When Lena began treatment she told me how she kept the few remnants of her father's life that she had been given by her mother in a special place in her flat. She spoke of these relics reverently, as if she had made her flat into a shrine to her father, so that in the stillness and deadness, paradoxically, she kept him alive. Indeed, she maintained a secret relationship with him, identifying with him and idealising their relationship as a dead couple. I put these ideas to her, and gradually she could see truth in them. As I further explored her love for her dead father, and with it her idealisation of death, she initiated a search in the official records, which led her to search through a lonely wood to find the place of his death, and then to visit the cemetery where his ashes were scattered. With the account of these events came an outpouring of pain and grief that startled and frightened her, the first breach in the sessions of her shell of self-control. After this, what I considered to be a normal period of mourning took its course over a number of months.

Following this period, she put away her father's mementos and redecorated her flat. At the time, I thought the treatment was a relatively straightforward case of arrested mourning in a neurotic patient, and I was impressed by Lena's capacity to face and mourn her loss. However, further analysis revealed she was not simply neurotic but had a much more disturbed, borderline personality. This was evident when a split-off, aggressive, omnipotent self entered the analysis, determined to have its own way.

Infant transference: being inside

As she relinquished links to her father, she turned to her original object—her mother—and began regressing, seeking a containing object in the transference. At the beginning of sessions she took the rug and wrapped it over and around her, although the weather was hot. When I interpreted this cocooning of herself as signifying her hope that I could contain her emotions and thoughts in the analysis, she rejected this interpretation. Instead she insisted the rug was me, warmly surrounding her, thus demonstrating her concrete thinking. I felt she was using sessions to promote the illusion she was inside me, safe and protected from separateness. Apparently she viewed object relations as being a situation where one is inside the other, as Britton (1998) has described, rather than consisting of two people communicating, sharing, understanding, and being understood. When I put this to her, she agreed, saying she had an image of climbing inside my body, struggling to fit in.

For many weeks, her sessions consisted of her lying in a warm, wrapped-up state, feeling blissfully at one with me. She felt content in this drowsy, cocooned state, often silent or speaking slowly of disconnected thoughts and memories. My interpretations of her wrapped-up state as a wish to be one with me, to be inside me, and not to see us as two separate people, to drift along in dreaminess, etc., did not seem to have much effect until eventually, after a time, she had a dream that seemed to break this mood. She dreamed that I took her upstairs to spend the night, tucking her up in bed like a child. Then, she had to go to the loo, which was outside, and she suddenly found herself at a busy crossroads where she found a toilet. Afterwards she was afraid she hadn't flushed the toilet properly, but the traffic prevented her from going back.

I took up this dream as her awareness that, although she wanted to be my baby, tucked up in bed in my house, at-one with me and safe inside me, she knew that when she left the session she was separate and outside, and this made her feel cross with me. In the busy traffic of her mind, wanting to protect me from her anger, she tried to flush the awareness of her anger down the loo, but was afraid it would not go down.

I also said that she was afraid that I would retaliate if she were cross with me. So she came to her session as if to a loo where she could produce the stuff and flush it down, do it properly. To this she responded that the dream summed up where we were: "I don't know my place, inside or outside, and I need boundaries. I don't want to go down some road that's depraved; I'm afraid I'll be uncontrolled." She could not tell me more about this fear, but it was to prove an insightful prediction.

The dream and its interpretation apparently dispersed the illusion of being inside me, for at the beginning of the next session Lena spoke in a grown-up way, saying she felt she was at a crossroads emotionally, in a dilemma about whether to make changes in her life or to go back, whether she had the guts to go forward in her life. I responded by saying that I thought she was referring to whether she had the guts to go on with the analysis. She responded: "I'm stuck in my life; I'm on a rocky path. I'm not a popular person, which makes everything worse, makes me want to draw back into the womb. My life has been so constricted, and now analysis has made me want to change. But what I really want is to come here to get love and all the things I didn't have when growing up, and it's like I refuse to go forward until I do. These are physical feelings, to be held, cuddled, to be taken care of like a baby, but you don't want to hear this. It's hard to speak of the sensations I have here. I want your body; that's what I missed out on, nice feelings like sun on the body, sucking your breast, baby feelings mixed up with adult. I've never been loved by anyone and I'm hungry for it."

Separation and the breast

The pre-oedipal transference became overt as she voiced her wish to be my baby. She admitted with shame that she fantasised at night and on the weekends that she sucked my breast, and that this fantasy "kept her going". At this point, I was unsure how to take this up, as the material might indicate that she was in a process of internalising me as a good feeding object or could be concretised wishes for nurture. However, I further thought about this as an auto-erotised fusion with me, fused and not separate, as if she owned my breast, taking its function as hers. I understood this as an attempt at omnipotent self-repair through a magical fulfilment of her neediness by the psychotic part of the self discussed by Bion (1957) and which Klein (1935) spoke of as a primitive defence against separateness and dependency. I settled on the idea that this was an omnipotent co-opting of the breast. I said to her that instead of having my words or interpretations inside her mind, at night she took my breast which was not attached to me or to here. Being here is different, I said, linking with thoughts and with words, two people speaking, listening, and understanding each other. I said that she took possession of my breast as if she owned it and then didn't need to depend on me the analyst as a person and the food of my interpretations. Without the illusion of owning and sucking my breast, I went on, she would have to experience my absence at night and on the weekends, and miss me. She replied that if I knew how much she fantasised sucking my breast, how she stole it and used it secretly, I'd go mad with anger.

Soon after this she had a dream that I felt was a direct consequence of the previous work on her phantasy of my breast: a dog had its teeth in the hand of a man. She hoped the dog would release the man's hand, but he told her that this would harm the dog. I interpreted this dream by saying that the hand stood for my breast and she believed that if she let go and was separate from me, she would be harmed. I said that she believed I wanted her to let go, that I was angry with her about her secret fantasy. In response, she said she wanted to give up the fantasy that she sucked my breast, which she knew was unreal and kept her from moving on. A few sessions later, she told me it had stopped, that she no longer wanted to come to soak up mothering and have a perfect, unchanging world here. She said, "I want you to acknowledge that I've changed, I've given up your breast. I don't know how it happened but it did." "But now," she went on, "I won't get anything. But if I didn't give it up, things would have got perverse. It wasn't real, though I made it seem real. The fantasy was keeping me from moving on, from having a relationship and friends." I said to her that she had given up the magic fantasy that my breast would fulfil all her needs; now she could have a different relationship with me, more real, not pretend, between two separate people.

In actual fact, I was unsure whether the relinquishment of her breast fantasy was real. I interpreted to her that she might have let it go because she believed I had pushed her away like her mother had done, because she thought I didn't want her hanging on, resentful of having to nurture her. To myself, I wondered if her putative relinquishment of the breast was due to compliance with what she thought I wanted, or actually a step out of fusion towards separateness.

Lena persisted in her belief she had relinquished the breast in order to move on, but instead of responding to my interpretations around mourning its loss, she expressed resentment about what she felt she had lost. This was made worse when, coming early to a session and seeing a male patient on my doorstep, she was painfully consumed with jealousy and anger, believing I gave him pleasures and nurturing denied to her. I said she thought that if there was anyone else in my life besides her, it meant I didn't care for her and withheld pleasures from her. I connected this to the birth of her younger sister, when she had experienced the loss of mother in having to share her. In the countertransference I felt the painful extent of this early trauma, how intolerable her sister's birth was for her. As I commented on this painful loss, her jealousy of my other patients, and her wish to exclusively possess me, she responded, "That's very basic, isn't it? I have given up your breast and I resent it. I'm afraid of what our relationship will be like now, that it will become destructive." A bit later she said jokingly that if she couldn't have an exclusive one-to-one relationship with me, she would kill me. Although this was said as a joke, a part of her was in deadly earnest, predicting we would live out a destructive relationship if she couldn't have her way.

As the interpretive work eroded her phantasies of one-ness with me, possession of the breast, and the desire for an exclusive relationship, she found separation increasingly difficult and expressed dread of the weekends. She said she hardly knew what to do with herself. "I'm waiting and waiting for you to do things for me. I can't do anything alone so I don't get on with my life." She told me she had never admitted to herself that she was lonely, always pretending she wasn't. She said, "I can't believe I'm saying this to you but I have to take responsibility for myself; you aren't going to give me everything I need. That's a terrible disappointment. The question is: will I or won't I do things for myself? No one wants me." I said, "When I don't supply everything you need, it means to you that I don't want you or like you." She said, "I need physical contact. I feel out in the cold now, alone. I was good, I gave up your breast and thought I'd be rewarded." In spite of her gloom, she had a good time over a Bank Holiday. When she returned she said she had missed me very much, but she soon regressed again, saying that she was afraid of what she would say to me and what would happen. She wanted me to hold her tight, to get on the couch and cuddle her. She had a fantasy of me getting on the couch with her, but the reason I didn't was because she was too unattractive. I said, "You believe I don't want you physically, that I cuddle other patients but not you." She said that if she were more attractive or thinner I would want her. She had thought analysis would give her a different body, smaller, shorter, thinner. I responded that she was centred on her body and couldn't think of herself as having a mind that connected with my mind. I said that there was a real misunderstanding between us, that if I didn't cuddle her, if we were separate, it meant I didn't want her and wanted to get rid of her. I said, "You want me to know how much you need physical affection." She said, "Yes, so much. It's hard to put into words, as if emotional contact is not enough, words and understanding are not enough. I think of you holding me and me melting into you. Then I could be carried around and not have to act, feeling safe and loved." I said, "It's so hard for you when I don't hold you physically. You would like to convert me to your view, to have me cuddle you."

Lena's feelings of abandonment when we separated on weekends increased. On Fridays she felt before her a yawning black gulf of emptiness that terrified her; all weekend she had suicidal thoughts and a painful yearning for me until Monday, when I would "bring her alive". The weekends meant rejection, as if I roughly pushed her away and ejected her. My efforts to help her be emotionally close, to contact her through understanding, to be her symbolic mother without our being concretely, physically intimate, did not take hold. Thus it was apparent that the omnipotent delusion that we were fused had ended, replaced by a phallic self that wanted to dominate. She threatened to burn her arm with an iron, to which I said she was burning with anger towards me for leaving her on the weekends, to which she said, "If I can't be the only one you want I'll make up miserable things to tell you; if I can't be you or just like you, I'll bring you down." I linked this with her dream of a flowered chamber pot full of poo and said, "It is like your dream that you could go on forever making poo and misery." She responded, "Yes, I can fill you up like all those figures in a Chagall painting, putting them into you. I see it that way, everything whirling around, filling you up to make you mine, with no room for anyone else." I responded that she wanted to take me over and control me, and make me pay for not cuddling her, putting bad feelings into me and believing she could get rid of them that way. She said, "I want to bring you to my level; if you feel bad just like I do, it makes me your responsibility." I said, "You believe that if I'm just like you and feel everything that you feel, I'll know you and exactly what to do for you." She said, "But there's a nasty side to wanting to fill you up with bad feelings—to get revenge on my mother. My adult life has all been about getting my own back on her." I felt hopeful that this piece of insight on Lena's part, that she was angry and vengeful towards her mother and was aware that she transferred this to me, was a positive sign that a shift towards the depressive position might take place along with guilt and reparation for the pain she inflicted.

Indeed, a long period of working-through the depressive position followed in which I felt we were becoming more of an analytic couple. Her more adult side alternated with her regressive determination to be infantile, with the delusion that she was only a body that needed to be looked after and filled up, feeling furious when she couldn't have the mothering she wanted. These states alternated, were reversed, and then reinstated, comprising a struggle with anal-sadistic phantasies which reiterated her love and hate for her mother. At times when she knew she was separate, she hated it; I spoke to her about how hard it was to feel separate, how empty her life felt, and how she couldn't imagine me liking her if we weren't exactly the same and at one. She would feel close to me for a little while but when I didn't fit in exactly with her view, hold her or cuddle her, she felt pushed away, or infuriated with me when she couldn't convert me to her point of view.

Magic, omnipotence, the narrow-track train, and the tiger

Around three years into the analysis, magical thinking began to further colour Lena's mental activity, reminding me of how Freud (1912–13) described a primitive, omnipotent belief that we "can alter the external world by mere thinking" and how Winnicott (1965) portrayed infantile omnipotence. At times, when she began to feel a bit better and more interested in the external world, she would make up her mind to do something, to go somewhere, to take a course, sign up for membership to an organisation, phone a friend, go on a diet, or get herself to bed earlier, but nothing would ever come of it. It became clear that for her the thought was equal to the deed, that all she needed to do was to think something and it would happen by itself. She was bewildered by this phenomenon, but denied my interpretations that it had to do with magical thinking or the fairy tales she had read as a child. She preferred to believe that she was weak or lazy, had lost her motivation, her "engine", or mostly that she needed me to be with her at home to help get her going. As it occurred again and again, she was gradually able to see what I meant and make more effort to carry her intentions through, but she continued to have difficulty sustaining efforts on her own behalf, expecting change through omnipotent projective identification, magically "becoming" the thing she wanted. This served to maintain a static, unchanging internal world in spite of a conscious wish on her part to make changes in her life.

Understanding her unconscious omnipotence made more sense to me of the peculiar passivity of her presentation, not fully accounted for by her often-voiced infant desire in the transference to be completely taken care of by me. I could understand better how the primitive phantasy was employed as a defence in childhood to deal with experiences of helplessness and terror, the fear of her parent's violence, trees falling, sibling rivalry, and her own anger. This defence enabled her to keep her mind still and the outside world under her magical control. Did the stillness she attempted to maintain in her internal world, I wondered, cover over and hide the uncontrolled and destructive aspects she had alluded to?

In her detailed studies of children in analysis, Klein (1935) observed that manic, omnipotent thinking served as a primitive defence against separateness, dependency, and envy. In both children and adults she saw how "torturing and perilous dependence on its loved objects drives the ego to find freedom" (1935, p. 277), engaging in manic activity to establish the self as free and in control. Klein characterised mania as the "utilization of the sense of omnipotence for the purpose of controlling and mastering objects ... in order to deny the dread of them" (ibid).

Lena's anxiety about our separateness was intense; if we were separate, she could lose me. Object loss appeared as her greatest fear at this time. Fusion, sameness, and magic were her preoccupations to defend against separateness, and a darker, more forceful tone began to prevail. A dream at the end of her third year in analysis showed a powerful manic process taking over her internal world. She dreamed there was an old-fashioned narrow-track railway. A train was rushing along at high speed through woods. She was on top of the train, frightened, having to duck to avoid branches of trees coming at her. There were logs on the track and other things that she was afraid would derail the train but they didn't. The fender, or the thing in front—she wasn't sure what it was called—was throwing them aside.

Her only association was to an earlier dream of not being in the driver's seat of her car. I took this up, saying that she believed the narrow-track train she was hurtling along on was out of her control and unstoppable; she was ducking and sweeping aside reality, especially my interpretations, with the fender of her mind. I interpreted this to mean that she was an old-fashioned girl who wanted to be looked after. On the narrow track of her determination to get me to agree, she pushed everything away to get me to do it her way. She continued to believe that I would reward her by making her wishes come true. I added that it was she who was driving this train of thought, sweeping aside reality, impervious to my interpretations, which could help her, not derail her. She responded by saying, "I can see it's my belief system, and that I think I'm right. I'm like Patient Griselda in a story I heard as a child." She told me that Patient Griselda was left by her husband, who was testing her faithfulness. Years went by, and she waited and waited for her husband to return. He returned and her virtue was rewarded. He put everything right. I said, "You believe you are married to me and you'll stay faithful until finally I put everything right for you. You stay on this narrow track, believe in the story, and sweep aside reality, fending it off. In waiting and waiting you believe you have the moral high ground; you'll get rewarded in the end, and not have to make efforts on your own behalf. You negate my functioning mind, which is not on a narrow track, but instead is free to think." She said, "You are my fairy godmother. I can see it's wrong but I won't give it up; it's my belief system." She was waiting for her life to be transformed by me, unable to tolerate depressive affect, reality, and the loss of her omnipotent beliefs and wishes.

Soon after this, she dreamed of a blind horse running with the bit between its teeth. Feeling the victim again, she reverted to complaining that she couldn't be part of my family on the weekends; she wanted me to "take her in". "I just want to suck your breast. I think you'll come over to me and give it." At this point I felt she was perverse: she knew that her fantasies were not real but nonetheless insisted on them. I felt she was bringing in more perversity because she felt more secure that I wouldn't act out with her. She told me of destructive fantasies, the wish to fill me up with a mushroom cloud that gets bigger and bigger, to suffocate me, to take over all the space, to push out other patients, to fill the room with a malignant presence; she said she wanted to show me the bad side of her. I said, "You are playing with fantasies but your hostility toward me is real. You hate that I am a separate person with thoughts that are different from yours. You think I'll come over to your point of view and be converted."

She missed a session then came saying she was afraid she would drive me mad or worse. She told me she had a very realistic dream two nights before that she was in the consulting room and sitting in the chair beside her was a large tiger. As she told me the dream, I felt a sense of menace; at this point I could grasp the intensity of the phantasy of having within her a powerful ferocity that could kill, representing her aggression, the fear at the heart of her pathology even more frightening than abandonment: omnipotent destructiveness that she was afraid she couldn't control, the angry tiger starved of love. I said, "You want me to know that I must take your destructiveness seriously and that you are frightened of these feelings." She said that she was afraid she might damage me. That I might commit suicide. As a child, she told me, she was often afraid her mother would kill herself as her father had done.

Before another long summer break, she had thoughts of stabbing her face with nail scissors while I was away, which I interpreted as her wish to stab me in the face, but instead turning her viciousness towards herself, aggressive feelings that she couldn't express directly towards me. I said that she didn't get overtly angry with me, wanting to keep me as a good object, and that she was afraid of her aggression, afraid the tiger in her would destroy me. In the first session after the break, Lena told me that she had had a good break, without any blackness. Then she told me a violent dream. She came into a room where someone was being shot and she had to wrestle a man to the ground. Stopping to think how to do it, she wondered whether to hit the side or front of his head. She chose the side, and bashed his head repeatedly on the ground. She had no associations to this dream. I took up the dream as a representation of the current analytic situation, how she felt hurt or killed by the break, and was angry with me, so wanted to come in, wrestle me down and finish me off in a sidelong way, secretly, as if she felt that we could not face her murderous feelings and understand them together. She responded with a thoughtful silence then said she was pleased with herself in the dream, she had stopped to think instead of going into action immediately.

Around this time, Lena began to express sadness about having made a mess of her life—the mistakes, the missed opportunities—manifesting a depressive quality. As she began to make changes to improve her external life, her sadistic phantasies intensified, as if the psychotic part of her mind had become inflamed by the threat of change. The atmosphere in the sessions before the winter break grew dark and malevolent as she told me of her admiration and eroticisation of violence. She spoke of how her father had snuffed out his own life, how she was fascinated with powerful, violent men such as Bluebeard, Tamburlaine, Genghis Khan, and also her stepfather, who was violent towards her mother; in these instances she could feel sexual excitement mixed with murder. She told me of frightening phantasies of being with a violent man, of killing a baby and then going to prison. Then she said, "I'm like a huge stubborn baby who won't grow up, who kills all that is not itself, greedy, nasty, and ugly. I've been afraid to tell you, but what I want is to be supreme, to have supremacy here … I kill off sparks of life that appear without my permission … any spontaneous creations." After this show of her hatred of otherness, she mounted an unrestrained omnipotent bid to take over the sessions with the single-minded force of the narrow-track engine in her dream.

Klein wrote of infant projective identification as "expelling dangerous substances (excrements) out of the self and into mother … expelled in hatred … to control and to take possession of the object" (1946, p. 8). Lena began to come in aggressively spoiling for a fight to establish "supremacy" and to colonise me. She told me I had been useless in helping her, insisting that I didn't care for her properly and that I was destroying her. Forcefully, she told me what to say and how I should be dealing with her, ordering me to put things in different places in my consulting room, to close the window, to dim the lights, demanding that I supply her with a weight-reducing diet, then felt angry and hurt when I didn't comply with her demands. Her projections and attacks made me feel helpless, unwanted, rejected, tormented, and angry. After I interpreted how she filled me with her bad feelings, hoping I could tolerate and understand them, she felt remorseful, worried about what she had inflicted on me, afraid that she would damage me or "bring me down". This concern showed she was able to empathise and I felt the remorse was genuine, but soon she would begin again, doing and undoing. She dreamed, in a strikingly symbolic (albeit concrete) portrayal of projective identification, of bringing large pieces of furniture in a van and moving them into my house. Her projections chilled me with their persistence and aggression, but I was hopeful there was movement in that her remorse and concern about me indicated her tolerance of the depressive position was strengthening.

Karate queen

Around five and a half years into the analysis, after more working-through in the transference, she had a dream that vividly revealed her destructive internal processes. She was alone in the middle of a large room. Then, people kept coming in through the window, one after the other; they besieged her. She picked up each one and threw them away, out the window, like a karate queen. In this dream, which I felt was another presentation of the manic omnipotence by which she maintained an empty psychic retreat (Steiner, 1993), she described an automatic impulse to throw out anyone or anything that entered her mind, allowing nothing to penetrate her; attacking her objects, her thinking, and her reflective capacities; crushing out any sparks of life that entered without her permission. In speaking to her I interpreted this was like a child throwing toys out of her pram, like rag dolls. Further, I said to her that this was how she kept her mind empty so that she didn't have to know what she felt or thought in relation to me. In this way she avoided both love and the anxiety of being invaded and taken over. Her obsession with order and cleanliness in her flat extended to keeping the house of her mind cleared out, in anal/sadistic evacuation, of anything she had not produced herself, narcissistically insulating herself from external influence and maintaining a psychic solipsism. The "karate queen" became a meaningful icon she and I often returned to in describing what she did to her objects and to my interpretations, rejecting any need or dependence on me or others.

Her persistent bids for supremacy eventually led to a turning point in the treatment, as I could no longer go on being taken over, bullied, and controlled. I took hold of my analytic prerogative and asserted my right to also be in the room, to have my own mind and to say my piece, which brought collisions with her bullying omnipotence. It became clear that as she dominated and filled the analytic space and tossed out or ignored whatever I said, the only way I could be heard was to interrupt her, which irritated and angered her. She then began to interrupt me, preventing me from speaking, and not listening. I would stop her, pointing out what was happening, how she wasn't listening to me, insisting on being able to finish my remarks, and in response to this she would become angry and argue loudly or withdraw in wounded rage. In my opposition to "takeover bids", as I stopped allowing myself to be ignored and controlled and struggled for my place, I kept in mind Britton's (2003) notion that narcissistic/borderline personalities need doses of "otherness" from the analyst to help them bear reality, and Segal's idea that psychic change requires "conflict, ambivalence and the attendant depressive anxiety" (1986, p. 216).

Lena continued to fill up the analytic space with her thoughts and to denigrate mine. She took differences between us as assaults. For example, when she came on a Monday to tell me a dream that she went on to interpret in her own way, a dark view of her plight, she was enraged when I suggested a different, as it happened, more positive interpretation of it, and would barely speak to me the rest of the session, complaining she felt misunderstood and pushed away. Using Steiner's (1993) analyst-centred interpretations, I pointed out that when she felt that I didn't completely agree with her and had different ideas of my own, she felt anxious that I was being critical or rejecting. I tried to make our differences more acceptable by saying, for example: "You feel anxious letting me in, afraid my ideas will take you over," or, "It's very difficult for you to bear considering my point of view, to hear what I have to say," or, "These are things you might be interested in knowing, my thoughts that can be taken in to join with your thoughts." At one point she responded with insight that she was aware she didn't listen to anyone. Teachers had told her that at school; she knew it was true and that she'd been that way all her life. With me, she said, there was more interaction than with anyone in the past. This, she said, included the two men she had had relationships with, where there was no real exchange; she had made herself into a slave to them, hoping to get something in return that she never got.

In working with Lena I had to trust the analytic process, difficult though it was with her. This required my holding onto the belief that it was necessary for her to undergo the pain of experiencing separateness, difference, and loss of omnipotence, and the frequent loss of equilibrium and disturbance that this entailed. Klein said of the loss of omnipotence:

> A decrease in omnipotence, which comes about with progress in integration and leads to some loss of hopefulness, yet makes possible a distinction between the destructive impulses and their effects; therefore aggressiveness and hate are felt to be less dangerous. (Klein, 1963b, p. 310)

Often after a session in which she argued with and attacked me, trying to prove I was wrong and she was right, insisting she knew best, Lena would come to the next session feeling meek and afraid that I would retaliate. Anxiously she then "put it right between us" by being contrite and remorseful for a short time, which she would soon undo again by arguing with something I said when I didn't agree perfectly with her.

Freud (1915c) described the splitting and oscillation between positions in the obsessional personality, between love and hate, compliance and defiance, doing and undoing. With each repetition in the transference, my interpretative work was directed towards linking these alternating states, aiming towards integration and working through the splits.

Internalisation of self-structure

Coming up to the long summer break at the end of the fifth year, I experienced a terrible struggle to help Lena internalise some goodness and to show her how she aimed her destructiveness towards the analysis whenever she was angry with me. I tried to show her how good experiences that occurred during the week were spoiled or devalued when she could not have me exclusively or be supreme. This occurred particularly around terrible anger and jealousy she felt after seeing another person leaving my house as she was arriving. Repeatedly I spoke to her about how difficult it was for her to feel she had to share me with others, how hard it was for her to keep alive in her mind anything good we had without allowing it to be destroyed.

Before and during the summer break I felt the usual disheartened pessimism about our work, but surprisingly she returned in a different state of mind, more reflective, sad about leaving it too late to have a child. Then a few months into the sixth year she had a dream of standing on a pier and looking into the sea. She said, "Under the water I could see buildings with two domes on them and I had feelings of contentment". I interpreted this dream to mean that she had found a firm place within herself to stand, and that there were good objects, breasts, under the surface inside her. At this point in the treatment I felt the struggles over the past few years and especially around the breaks had helped her to internalise some ego structure and an aspect of me as a nurturing maternal object, robust enough to bear her aggression and not so likely to abandon her.

Lena gradually began to use sessions in a more ordinary way to speak of problems around work, family, and her struggles with herself. In other words, by giving up omnipotence she gained ordinary potency and the capacity to think. Externally, she began to stand up for herself at work and effectively fight her corner, not allowing herself to be walked over as she had before beginning analysis; she spoke of this as "finding a self". In spite of her complaints about the mess that other people made when they visited—crumbs on the floor, washing up to do, etc.—she began to see more of friends and relatives, inviting them around to her newly purchased home, tolerating their otherness. She told me she hoped to meet someone, to find a partner, and she spoke tentatively of dates with men. I should mention here that the difficulty in being in the consulting room with her was mitigated all along by something basically likeable and honest in her.

Progress and integration were slow, a more apparently consolidated self-state was often quickly followed by a vicious attack on herself or me, using suffering as an omnipotent means to triumph over the side of her that was able to develop and relate to life (Joseph, 1983) and to avoid guilt and reparation (Riesenberg-Malcolm, 1981). She told me of a dead blackbird she had found in her garden that she had tenderly and sadly wrapped in newspaper and laid in her rubbish bin. The next day she was startled and delighted by a live blackbird on her windowsill that she much preferred to the dead one—possibly an instance of magical reparation, yet still an illustration of how life and death battled within her, and in this instance, life appeared to have won.

Discussion

In the first stage of treatment, Lena was able to mourn the loss of her father, with acute sadness, then put away his mementos. Turning towards the maternal object, she regressed, attempting to live inside, to fuse with, and to be at-one with the analyst, denying separateness. To experience analyst and patient as two separate people meant she would be dependent on an object she could lose, which was intolerable for this traumatised girl. Regressive fantasies, separation anxiety, and attempts to control the analyst followed, together with magical thinking and omnipotence, hidden aggression, and destructiveness in a bid for power over the analyst.

As Freud (1930a) and Rosenfeld (1971) suggested, there is pleasure in destructive omnipotence for its own sake. Often I felt that Lena experienced the sheer pleasure of wielding power in her identifications with the figures of omnipotent baby, supreme bully, narrow-track train, Chagall filling up all the space, perverse destructive fantasies, and the karate queen, in a manic/obsessive effort to control me, the primal object, in the transference. During the later period of her analysis, her resolve to have "supremacy" felt like an urge to triumph not only over me but over life itself, as she repeatedly destroyed her own intentions towards positive change and her experience of me as a good, helpful object. I think this was powerfully connected to her libidinal-sadistic cathexis of death and its link to her oedipal love for her dead father.

When I could no longer allow her to take over the sessions, insisting on my right to be in the room and to be heard, I became a firmer target for her aggression. This instigated repeated cycles of angry attacks, loss and recovery of equilibrium, retreat, remorse, and reparation in the form of contrition. The presentation of myself as "other" and separate, whether in relation to weekends and breaks, or being a presence in the room with something to say, was often unbearably persecutory for her. Britton (1998, 2003) has said of narcissistic/borderline personalities that they are people for whom anything that isn't *self* is persecutory: they are difficult to contain babies, as if they have a milk allergy, a negative reaction to foreign protein and say, "No—I can't possibly take anything in". Britton has argued that the task of the analyst is to inoculate the patient to a tolerance of the foreign protein of otherness and to reality outside the self; the analyst must do this by helping the patient to listen, to take in and to remember what was said in sessions in order to slowly build up their tolerance of otherness.

The psychotic aspect of narcissistic and borderline functioning, in which there is a powerful, aggressive attempt to get the other to conform to his or her internal reality, is widely recognised, for example by Bell (2002). As Lena and I collided repeatedly and sometimes tempestuously in the transference relationship, her capacity to tolerate otherness and difference increased and her relationship to the realities of her life improved. In becoming less frightened of her own aggression and working it through in the transference, she was able to stand up for herself at work and in relation to her mother. She bought a house with a garden, which she had always wanted. She eventually expressed gratitude that I was able to bear her attacks and projections, and felt sorry about how difficult she had been.

Lena's analysis revealed the malignant destructive unconscious phantasies together with magical thinking that so frightened her, the admiration for murderous figures such as Bluebeard and Genghis Khan and her desire to command and destroy that appeared to be pleasure in destructiveness for its own sake. Although to some degree Lena's narcissistic organisation was defensive against maternal loss, it also contained the terrifying romance with death that was within her. Freud (1930a) said of the death instinct that it carries out its destructiveness silently within the self, and "escapes detection unless its presence is betrayed by its being alloyed with Eros", suggesting the notion that destructiveness towards "some other thing", as he put it, enables preservation of the self. Clinically, I take this to mean that within the libidinal analytic relationship, tolerance and working-through of aggressive phantasies allow the self to strengthen, as it did with Lena, becoming freer from internal undermining, superego self-punishments, and terror of aggression.

As we know, Freud was pessimistic about the degree to which destructiveness can be modified by psychoanalysis (1930a). However, clinically, instinctual transformation and integration is dependent on the analyst's willingness to engage with instinctual negativity and destructiveness, together with the part played by remorse and gratitude emphasised by Klein (1957).

In the next chapter I will describe the defensive narcissistic organisations in two patients whose unconscious psychotic phantasy in relation to their object could be distinguished and analysed.

CHAPTER FIVE

Non-consummation: a narcissistic organisation

On observing a particular emotional pattern in many of my patients, my interest has been provoked by the phenomenon of holding back and letting go, and the sense of gratification in having power over these functions. In an everyday sense, withholding or giving can be used as a means of influence and control, of reward and punishment. Psycho-analytically, the importance of this phenomenon, initially noted by Freud (1905d) in the *Three Essays*, was formulated as an interest and pleasure in defecation and urination—in expelling and holding in—and featured as an expression of self-will or defiance by the small child towards the parent.

This body-based model, shaped by the physiological/social development of the child, remains, according to Freud, in the unconscious as a mental configuration of early complex object relations, as emotions, thoughts, and actions, which express themselves in adulthood in various ways. I will use these ideas to understand two distinctive cases of withholding, neurotic patients, demonstrating the way in which they formed defensive narcissistic organisations to protect themselves from terrifying psychotic anxieties in relation to the other.

When Freud (1908b) wrote about anal-erotism linked with sadism and furthermore about the anal character traits of orderliness, parsimony, and obstinacy, he was offering a model based on insights from clinical observation and human experience. He also studied reaction formations against the interest in defecation, such as shame, fastidiousness, and extra-kindliness—mechanisms used to oppose the desire to make a mess or to counteract anal aggression and sadomasochism. An example from my practice was a man who used an anal character formation to withhold his desire to make a destructive anal mess. After three years of working with his politeness, his cleanliness, and his bland presentation as the "good patient", he had several dreams indicating that the containing function of his character traits had leaked or been broken through, letting out his mess and aggression in the form of forgotten shameful memories and frightening fantasies.

Abraham (1921, p. 379) wrote of the way in which anal fixations impair masculine potency, as was the case in the above patient. Writing at length on anal characters, Abraham (1924, pp. 425, 430) noted their manner of giving or presenting something: they refuse to give on demand or request, holding back until the time of their own choosing. More recently, the psychoanalytic literature has been filled with illustrations and examples of anal-type expulsion of unwanted mental contents in acts of projective identification. Abraham saw the anal phase as divided into two different parts according to the conduct towards the object: in the first, anal-erotism is linked to evacuation of sadistic impulses aimed towards destruction of the object. In the second phase, by contrast, anal pleasure is gained by retention, holding back, and sadistic impulses are satisfied by possessive control of the object. As Abraham showed, destructive attacks on the object can be seen to alternate with attempts to possess and control. Both correspond to the basic function of the anal sphincter.

I wish to emphasise that this is equally true in regard to the urethral sphincter and, in fact, applies to all erotic zones of the body whereby erotic pleasure can be gained by means of retention and release. Metaphorically, its use is limitless. Freud (1905d), Abraham (1920), Fenichel (1945), and Klein (1932) have all noted that urination—its retention and expulsion—can be observed in connection to phantasies of aggression and destruction. This situation could be seen in the analysis of the first patient I wish to discuss, Charles, in whom the destructive power of urine and the fear of unleashing it was a central phantasy.

Charles

Charles was a thirty-two-year-old man who worked in a professional field. He was socially isolated when he began analysis and had never had a relationship of any kind with a woman, though he felt himself to be heterosexual. My impression of his family was that they were particularly emotionally constipated, unable to tolerate expression of feelings in a general sense. Charles was sent to boarding school at age seven, against his mother's wishes, with no preparation or understanding of what this would mean. His sense of abandonment was catastrophic and he gave me a recurrent, heartbreaking image of a boy who did not wish to burden his mother with his distress. Every time his parents left him at school or visited him, he waited until they had gone home and the lights were put out in the dormitory to let out his racking sobs, stifling them in his pillow, feeling devastated and betrayed by his abandonment. Night after night, he told me, he would stifle his sobs until they were blotted out. He refused food at school, only nibbling at the food in the tuck box under his bed in the dormitory. Charles had an eating disorder throughout childhood and as an adult he had little appetite for food, as if all his appetites and desires had been beaten down and denied expression, along with his tears.

Having had experience of a previous therapy, Charles took easily to free association, introspecting and reporting his thoughts about his life, his conscious fantasies about me, about himself, and about the analytic situation. Initially he appeared to be a perfect patient, with fine manners and co-operative speech.

In my countertransference, however, I soon began to experience a powerful deadness and lack of emotional contact. Then he dreamed of himself as a boy in a yard surrounding a large institutional building with numerous other children. In the dream he was desperate to urinate and frantically looked for somewhere to relieve himself but he could find no place to go. The pressure was escalating and he felt he would burst. He went along the iron railings around the school grounds and found a break in them, where the bicycles were kept, through which it was possible to slip out. Beyond the railings he could see green fields and a lake that looked peaceful and inviting, but he was not able go out and he continued pacing up and down the yard. His associations to the dream were to boarding school and how imprisoned he felt there. I interpreted his needing to urinate as the pressure to let out the powerful emotions of neediness, rage, and loss that had filled him when his parents left him at school. These were emotions that he had smothered and deadened in his pillow at night, but were still alive within him. I said that he wanted to find a place to put them but was unsure whether analysis was a place safe enough for him to let them out and relieve himself.

The dream, I said, was telling us in the present time that he could leave the school that had imprisoned him as a child, release his emotions, and escape his torment.

His associations to the dream also revealed that the alluring fields and lake beyond the railings represented his mother, forbidden to him by his father's banishment to boarding school, as well as his great fear of opposing his father's regime by linking up with his mother as the desirable good object. Urination in the dream represented both a forbidden oedipal pleasure and a violent attack on the primal scene, which he had to hold back and control. As I interpreted the dream, as above, I felt it explained the deadness I felt in the countertransference, a result of the barrier he kept between us, that is, his active attack on any emotional link with me as a representative of the forbidden oedipal mother, jealously possessed by a frightening father. He smothered any possibility of liveliness in our relationship and he attempted to control my liveliness by making me non-existent. When he killed me off, he would not be tempted to gain maternal sustenance from me and at the same time, he would omnipotently keep me safe from his dangerous feelings, his anger and distress.

Bion (1962) held that there are three fundamental links to objects: love, hate, and knowledge, which he schematised as L, H, and K. He then suggested that the negative of these attachments existed; –L, –H, and –K. My patient, one could see, was initially in –L, –H, and –K. He wanted neither to love nor to hate; he wanted to know nothing of his objects and any features they had that would affect him or attract him. If he were to escape from his position of extreme continence within the safety of the railing fence, his narcissistic organisation, he feared the desire and rage within him would gush out with uncontrolled force, damaging and overwhelming himself and me, and once started, he feared it would never stop.

Other dreams followed that confirmed his psychotic phantasy of losing everything inside him: he dreamed of peeing endlessly and then, of crying endlessly, frightening dreams that expressed his terrible fears of incontinence, representing a perpetual loss of internal security and a lack of containment. As I spoke to him about how frightened he was to talk to me about his anxieties and fearful emotions, he eventually discovered that his analysis was safe enough to contain his feelings. He began to let go and find his previously inhibited emotional life, exploring his feelings and associations as they arose in the sessions. These included being in touch with his rage as a child and a positive oedipal transference to me, which enlivened the analysis and eventually enabled him to become engaged to be married. Finally, he could inhabit his life as a potent male.

Ms B

My second patient, Ms B, a woman from abroad who began her analysis in her thirties, seemed ostensibly very different from Charles: from the very beginning she made no attempt to hold back her criticisms of me, her aggressive attacks, or her contempt. Instead, it was any positive feelings that were retained and defended against; she loathed any feeling or expression of need, love, or dependency. Ms B had grown up in a family in which there was not enough love or other resources to go around, so she felt unloved, nobody's favourite, and that nothing that was available was quite good enough.

Ms B was troubled by her aggressive tendencies and conflicts with her partner, co-workers and friends. She wanted to be liked or loved, yet made it difficult or impossible for others to like her. During the first years of her analysis, coming four times a week, her spontaneous comments often consisted of withering criticisms of my décor or objects in my consulting room and, not least, my interpretations. She treated herself no better. The stories she told me about herself consistently displayed herself in a bad light; she berated and criticised herself, as if she should never find pleasure in feeling good about herself or any of her accomplishments. She used the sessions perversely and masochistically, insisting on suffering, reiterating her grievances, telling me she was naturally aggressive and that was that, nothing could be done about it. I was meant to watch helplessly and to bear the feeling that nothing I said made much difference. We both agreed that she was envious, probably of everyone, and this made it difficult for her to accept anything nourishing from me or anyone else, as that would mean others had something to give that she couldn't give herself, which would undermine her determined self-sufficiency. She complained she wanted a new analyst, that others got support that she didn't get from me. Her contemptuous and destructive attacks on me and the analysis went on and on for some months. She often despaired of not being able to enjoy anything she was given, keeping herself stripped and bare, re-enacting a childhood in which she felt she had nothing, unable to dispose of any of the miseries from her past or take in anything good in the present.

Then the quality of her sessions changed: anal retentiveness came to the fore. She came with decisions she had to make, large and small, around which she would discuss the pros and cons, over and over, in session after session, unable to make choices. After researching on the internet for hours and finally placing an order for something she needed, she could not press the "Confirm" key and finalise the choice; she held back, "kept it all on the table", as she put it. Suffering loss of the items unchosen was part of it; however, it became clear that the hectic excitement of having the possibilities "on the table" was the crucial element. If and when she did finally press "Confirm", she felt a sense of anticlimax and was no longer interested in the piece of furniture, the holiday, or the gift she had chosen. The avid desire had disappeared. Further material revealed more. Ms B described her relationship to food: she anticipated a meal, holding an image in her mind of a delicious dinner, holding on to the desire and the longing for it, but when she actually ate the food, she couldn't allow herself the experience of eating, the pleasure of it. When it was over and gone, she felt sad and deprived.

A crucial revelation came when Ms B told me that she and her partner, though presently rarely having sex, had established a particular pattern in their sexual activities during their first year together: their passion for each other had been powerful; they made love for hours, reaching a high level of arousal over several days, withholding climax, until finally, when it became unbearable, they let go and allowed orgasm. Afterwards, Ms B's reaction was profound. She felt hugely downcast, depressed, disappointed. His sexual desire had abated; he no longer wanted her; the tension was gone. The *petit mort* was felt to be a real death. To delay this crash landing, maintaining a feeling of power, her model of sexuality was to prolong excitement as long as possible: nonconsummation instead of consummation as the perpetual gratification.

Then I realised she was applying the same model to her analysis, holding back, preventing progress, since becoming better would end the analysis and she would no longer be wanted by me. When I said this to her, she responded, "Yes, better the journey than to arrive." This model further explained why her analysis was stalled, why she taunted, criticised, and teased me: she wanted to maintain an aroused state of desire without consummation. Thus, she ignored my interpretations and refused to take them in, enjoy them, or use them; in this way altering psychoanalysis from an oral, feeding model to a sexual, genital model. This meant she didn't get nourished, couldn't metabolise, and didn't learn. Instead, the constant feeling in the countertransference was that I was to excite her, to provide stimulation, to turn her on, to touch her in the right spot and to maintain the aroused state of desire, but not actually to satisfy her. However, my words were forever falling short of being thrilling enough. She kept herself in a psychic retreat (Steiner, 1993) of non-consummation, waiting for me to provide the elusive climax, leaving me feeling frustrated and leaving her unanalysed.

Ms B's determination to hold on to the state of non-completion could be further understood by examining its importance as a defence. Keeping surrender at bay in her transference to me, in which I was to feel frustrated and unsatisfied without the possibility of an alive libidinal connection, she kept away the risk of object loss and the disastrous phantasy of losing herself in the object. The dynamic of her sexual relationship with her partner was to project her desire into the man, making his post-coital loss of libido feel like a catastrophic loss of her own sexuality as well, the intense passion she equated with the life force. This loss of vitality associated with the disappearance of sexual desire is, in both men and women, a fear more profound than fear of castration, according to Ernest Jones (1927), who introduced the term *aphanisis* in describing it. This is a fear both sexes have in common; however, in men it has the significance of castration while in women it takes the form of abject feelings of separation and loss of the loved object. Described by Jones as equivalent to loss of the self and death, *aphanisis* is the ultimate catastrophe.

Jones's idea throws light on the imperative for some personalities to develop an organised defence of non-consummation as a retreat and a self-protection. Why this would be so intensely clung to, given *aphanisis* equals death, may indicate the strength of the unconscious psychotic anxiety at its core. The terror defended against by the pathological organisation in Ms B was further demonstrated in the patient's material when she angrily told me on several occasions, "You want me to surrender to my emotions, to let go and confess love and need for you. If I did that I would liquefy, flow into you, and be lost and disappear." She dreamed after the summer break of going to the loo and, looking into the bowl, saw all her lifeblood there, about to be flushed away. Her unconscious psychotic phantasy was the fear of loss of identity and self, the release of an emotional flow that would drain her of herself.

Discussion

Both Charles and Ms B established narcissistic organisations based on an anal pattern of retention, forming psychic retreats making them "difficult-to-reach" patients. At the heart of their predicament were horrifying unconscious psychotic anxieties that prevented consummation of their desires.

For Charles, if he let go, tears and urine would flow, emptying him out. As long as he could restrain the flow, he imagined he could keep his objects and himself safe inside. Releasing urine and tears involved the terrifying phantasy of endless loss, a never-ending emptying-out of mental contents and self.

Ms B similarly imposed an anal pattern onto the genital and the psychoanalytic situation. Her presentation was genital in libidinal desire and location, but anal in style and expression. The terrifying unconscious psychotic phantasy powering her defences was a complete loss of her identity, of her separate self and her volition, lost in the flux, given over to my will and control. So frightened of this phantasy was she that she maintained a psychic retreat of non-consummation, not allowing love, affection, pleasure in friendship, sexual enjoyment, self-respect for her many accomplishments, or the consummation of our analytic relationship. She defended her retreat with intellectualisation, aggressive criticisms of me, and the spoiling of my interpretations and therefore of the analysis. To allow her feelings to flow meant emotional contact with her objects, which she feared would be loss of herself and the catastrophic realisation of her worst anxieties. As we spoke of these things, I said, "You hold back and don't let yourself have what you want in your life." She responded evocatively, "I've never really turned up for my own life." In speaking of her difficulties in thinking, she lit upon an acute insight: "To process is to evacuate, to lose everything," telling of the power of her terrifying phantasy that we were struggling to make clearer through analysis of her dreams and associations.

It is interesting to think about the difference between the two patients in the form of the substance they imagined would be lost. Losing fluids could be equated with losing blood and bleeding to death in the unconscious, while losing solids would be more a fear of losing objects, a fear of unrequited love, as could be seen in Ms B's case, together with loss of self as object.

Bion's idea of the container/contained has great relevance to the understanding of both my retentive, non-consummating patients. Each constructed a defensive pathological organisation between the paranoid/schizoid and depressive position designed to contain their psychotic anxiety. As Bion wrote of a patient, "he was trying to contain himself, as someone says of someone about to lose control of himself; he was trying to 'contain' his emotions … as one might speak of a general attempting to 'contain' enemy forces within a given zone" (1970, p. 94). Conceiving of a container outside the self that would be able to hold the devastating flow, or stem the tide that threatened to empty or destroy them, was felt to be impossible. It would be difficult to comprehend this psychic situation without considering it to be due to a failure of the container/contained relationship with the mother.

Melanie Klein described early primitive object relations and ego disturbances as resulting from excessive projective identification, so that the projection of parts of the infant into the mother occurs to an immoderate degree. The infant then feels it is a self trapped concretely in the object, and the essential communicative function of projective identification is lost. Rosenfeld (1965), working with psychotic patients, became familiar with their phantasies: he wrote of the fear of projective identification in these patients whenever they approached an object with love or hate. "The patient said, 'If one goes all the way one cannot retake everything.' I then interpreted that when he loved somebody and believed in him or her, he wanted to go all the way, which meant to him that he went inside the other person and so he got mixed up and confused. He also felt that when he put himself into people he had difficulty in taking himself out again … as he feared he would not only lose me but himself. He agreed wholeheartedly … and said, 'A big-boned man eats a lot' and he made chewing movements" (1965, p. 114). Of another of his patients, Rosenfeld wrote, "Only very gradually could he admit more of his own interest in me, but as there was also a reciprocal fear of his forcing himself, or falling into me, any expression of affection was usually followed by fears of getting entangled inside me" (ibid., p. 49). Another patient said, "'One has to find one's own roots. I do not know whether it is right liking you too much.' I interpreted that he was afraid that by liking me too much he would get right inside me and lose his own roots and himself" (ibid., p. 110).

Furthermore, Bion is helpful in describing the fear of the containing object. Speaking in an abstract way about the unconscious phantasy of the malignant container, he says, "The theory is that an object is placed into a container in such a way that either the container or the contained object is destroyed. In pictorial terms the container is represented by a mouth or vagina, the contained by a breast or penis" (1970, p. 109). Ms B's particular phantasy was that she would be sucked into the container as into a greedy mouth and then entrapped, absorbed, and disintegrated. Her concern and anxiety was for her safety, not concern for the object, and thus her anxiety was paranoid/schizoid in nature, although depressive concern was to appear as the work continued. Charles withheld urine as it contained his frustration and aggression, which he believed would be dangerous for the good object that he wanted to preserve, manifesting depressive anxiety. In his state of depressive anxiety, his love and genital urges and his hate and sorrow were all mixed up; thus his L, H, and K were intertwined and intermeshed, negated and not projected. He wanted to protect his mother from painful projections and feared that his love for her would bring wrath from his father. The lovely lake and landscape outside the school grounds that beckoned was a Garden of Eden forbidden to him, a symbolic version of the contact he was denied with his mother by a possessive, threatening father. In both cases, for Charles and Ms B, the defensive organisation was narcissistic in nature, in that it protected the self and its internal contents from being drained out and lost, but as a consequence prevented relationships and emotional contact with others.

The quality of non-consummation granted by the narcissistic organisation in my patients was itself gratifying in that it provided a sense of power and control, an orientation to the world and the self that harboured and controlled a dangerous phantasy. This made the work in the transference slow and intermittent, requiring long but rewarding analyses. Both analyses, though they provided a much needed attachment object, were threatening to the patients, as the power of the positive transference always threatened the possibility of the loss of self into the object.

The narcissist meets with obdurate factors in their identity that prevent closeness and object love. Britton has discussed narcissism in relation to an innate hostility to object relations, a phenomenon he termed "psychic atopia", the will to eliminate otherness that blocks and confounds intimate relationships. This will be discussed in the next chapter.

CHAPTER SIX

The other as alien: psychic atopia

There are many reasons why individuals have difficulty connecting with others. In Chapter Four I discussed a woman who omitted relationships from her life, stayed alone, and kept all stimuli at bay because of terror of her destructive omnipotent phantasies. In Chapters Three and Five, I discussed patients whose withdrawal to narcissistic organisations prevented closeness to others which they felt could diminish, damage, or even threaten their lives. The wish to keep others out may be due to less extreme origins such as shyness, an introverted personality, paranoid states, or envy; for many, painful experiences with previous relationships or life situations have left a residue of shame, guilt, or humiliation making new relationships problematic.

This chapter will address the more difficult end of the spectrum. After a period of psychoanalytic work, when the patient has gained some trust in the method and in the analyst, and has been relieved of some of his symptoms, a plateau can be reached in which the analyst has difficulty making meaningful emotional connection with the patient and the patient has difficulty listening and taking things in from the analyst. Although emotional closeness may be something the patient consciously desires, still the patient keeps a certain distance and prevents contact, as if the other is alien. How can we understand this? There appears to be some unconscious element that opposes intimacy and contact.

Britton (2003) has introduced the concept of *psychic atopia*, which takes a view on what these deep resistances or disconnections might be. In his theory, Britton suggests that there exists a psychological allergy to otherness and to the products of other minds, similar to a biological allergy, that makes comprehensible why the other is kept at a distance. He proposes that there is an innate factor at work in the infant that is aversive to contact and says "no" to otherness, and that this exists to a degree in all of us. If this is so, it has a particular significance for mother–baby relationships, indicating that it is not only the non-containing or absent maternal object that produces an anxious, uncontained infant, but that an innate factor within the infant may be the problem. This factor may account for the disappointing situation of stalemate or impasse sometimes reached in analyses. I will illustrate the concept with clinical material from two patients who I believe had this reaction to otherness at a deep level. I propose to extend Britton's idea of an allergic reaction to otherness to suggest that this primitive negative response to otherness predates envy and narcissism, although Britton classifies these patients as narcissists. That is, psychic atopia describes an *a priori* pre-object, pre-symbolic position at the foundation of infant life that contributes to the development of narcissism and narcissistic structures. It is not Freud's primary narcissism, but is the same phenomenon that Freud observed, I think, when he said that hate is prior to love, a situation in which the primordial self is without territorial borders and is inhospitable to otherness.

Britton elaborates the effects of his *psychic atopia* in two groups of patients. The first of these he terms the hyper-subjective patient who wants complete "oneness" with the analyst, seeking a relationship of two people with one mind, or treats the other as an extension of self. In this patient, the analyst notices a hypersensitivity to criticism, to his objective gaze or any objective appraisal; above all, the analyst notices how the patient rejects any interpretations from a third position. The second group of patients, whom he calls the hyper-objective, are people who avoid intersubjectivity altogether; they fear invasion by the other and losing their psychic integrity, demonstrating a negative reaction to linking emotionally with the other. Such patients are schizoid in type and prefer an objective, intellectual relationship with their objects, essentially setting up a situation of two separate people unable to connect.

Following Rosenfeld (1987), Britton uses his terms of "thin-skinned" and "thick-skinned" narcissism to further describe these types.

In spite of their apparent differences, both groups have an aversion to otherness at a deep level, but with different configurations. The hyper-subjective patient requires his object to be an all-embracing mother, to have perfect understanding of him and perfect oneness, as exemplified by his ideal maternal relationship. An example of this type is Sarah, the first patient I will present below. In contrast, the hyper-objective person requires his object to remain at a distance, free of emotional relating, and consistently brings into the relationship a third view that personifies objective intellectual knowledge, representing the non-personal, meaning-giving father; my second patient, George, is an example of this type. I would like to make the point that, although they appear to be different, both types suffer from the same phenomenon: a terror of penetration into their psychic space. The hyper-subjective's bid to live inside the object exhibits the same desire as the hyper-objective person: to remain intact, whole and unpenetrated by foreignness. This has a meaning in relation to the physical body and sexuality, but in particular to the mind and its function of taking in and digesting new ideas.

Others have written about phenomena similar to the atopia Britton describes. It appears that André Green (2002) is addressing a contiguous or similar area when he discusses his "central phobic position". He speaks of problems around a refusal to introject and the rejection of reality that manifests as disturbances in free association; its aim is to protect and occlude a vulnerable "central core area of psychic functioning". In Green's theory, there is phobic avoidance of this core area, which, if contacted, would make links and connections that would lead to a psychic catastrophe, a vortex of terror and meaninglessness. Similarly, Hanna Segal (1986), Roy Schafer (1997) and Henri Rey (1994) wrote about patients with blocked or faulty introjection, who manifested a refusal to take anything in. Gianna Williams (1997) designated the term "no-entry system" for defences against penetration in patients whose container/contained relationship with the mother has failed and who often become anorexic. She suggested these patients had been penetrated by toxic projections from the mother. The patients described by these writers maintain a defensive non-introjective position to guard the self against bad, persecutory, or intrusive projections from objects. These conceptualisations link with Fonagy's (1991) argument in relation to narcissistic/borderline patients: the notion that they cannot tolerate the close presence of other objects, that is, the situation where two minds exist in the same space at the same time. Finding the analytic situation unbearable, they are driven to defensive positions, that is, to merge with the analyst or to take flight into distance, or to quote Fonagy and Target (1994), "to nullify his mental existence" in other ways.

Henri Rey, writing of the phantasy of fusion with the object says: "The fear of separation from the object and the desire to penetrate into it and fuse with it into a primal unity can be so intense that it surpasses human understanding" (1994, p. 13). Rey, Klein, and others argue that projective identification is employed defensively against fears of separation. However, I am arguing here, reflected in the clinical material below, that a prior factor is at work that is even more fundamental. For these patients, fusion or distance defends against a mortal terror of being penetrated and taken over, as if contact with non-self at primitive levels is antithetical to survival at an early stage of development. While Britton conceptualises this as immune incompatibility, I suggest it can also be seen as primitive hatred, the fear of intrusion into a developing core self, operating before object love is experienced, the remnants of which remain in adult relationships. Rosenfeld (1987) makes reference to projections from the mother possibly occurring when the foetus is still in utero, which in a mysterious way finds its way into the child:

> This process continues after birth and prevents the child from form-
> ing a normal relationship to the mother … children of this kind
> are from the beginning of life phobic about their mother. They are
> terrified that they may at any moment have to guard against some-
> thing very frightening which is being forced into them. They need
> to block the mother's influence; this can be observed after the child
> is born but sometimes it starts immediately after birth and gives
> rise to severe feeding disturbances and the tendency to turn away
> from contact with the mother. (1987, p. 276)

Britton (2003) writes of the effect on the container/contained relationship between infant and mother of what he considers an innate atopic phenomenon:

> Is there *an innate factor* in the infant that increases the risk of *a failure*
> *of maternal containment*, and, if so, what might it be? … I believe

there is and I have come to think of it as a kind of *psychic atopia*, a hypersensitivity to psychic difference, an allergy to the products of other minds.... I believe this variable in the individual constitution, the psychic counterpart to the tolerance and intolerance of the somatic immune system, may contribute to difficulties in infantile containment. (2003, p. 177, Britton's italics)

Sarah

I would like to present some clinical material to illustrate this phenomenon from a long four-times-weekly analysis of a hyper-subjective woman who was in her thirties and forties over the time of her analysis.

Sarah, as I shall call her, was the first child born into a professional family. The family story around her birth was that for the first two years of her infancy she cried non-stop and no amount of holding and rocking would comfort her, driving her mother round the bend. Mother tried hard to care for her but was unable to, even with father's help and encouragement. When Sarah's younger brother was born eighteen months later, and her sister born a few years after that, mother was able to look after them and to enjoy mothering. Even taking into account the patient's exaggerations, and the probability of the mother's difficulty with a first baby, Sarah could only be described as a "difficult-to-contain" baby.

In the early stages of analysis, she wanted to be close to me, and for a time this was possible and she felt understood as she told me of her life. Then, as we began to go more deeply into things, we entered a long and painful period in which, in the transference, she pushed me away and attempted to take control of the process, demanding that I respond in just the way she wanted. She took up the position that she knew best how to conduct her analysis, and when I didn't agree completely or give her just what she wanted, she would go into rebellious silences or attack me for not understanding her. It was as if there was an anorexic part of her that would rather starve than eat my food or accept my maternal influence.

Sarah's dreams began to reveal unconscious desires: she dreamed of being inside me, concretely inside my body, and had many dreams of twins and Siamese twins. One was a vivid dream of identical twins who were ice-skating, entwined in an erotic dance, fascinating to her as they moved their arms and legs together as if they were one body and one person. These dreams appeared during a period in which she was expressing anger towards others for having things she wanted, and particularly towards me for what she felt I possessed and she didn't have. Envy, as we know, can sometimes be worked with, made less inflammatory, and may develop into a tolerance for bearing differences, but I had a strong sense that Sarah found differences intolerable and tried to make us into twins, equal and identical. Thus, she maintained the illusion that we were the same person but not, as I had first believed, as a defence against envy, hatred, or anxiety; instead, it felt different, as if she hated otherness itself, preventing closeness in the analytic relationship that could enable working-through and reparation. The transference, I thought, was a repetition of the early battle with her mother, pushing me away and at the same time furious that we weren't one, demanding control and oneness to deny my separate existence. To give a sample from the work in the thick of it with her, during a difficult period, Sarah began a Friday session angrily:

[Sarah abbreviated as S. Analyst abbreviated as A.]

S: I didn't feel looked-after yesterday. I don't feel you care about me. You didn't analyse my dream properly. [She'd dreamed about a red car that she had taken to a garage to trade in for a better one and had been given a rusty, old car.] You said I wanted to trade you in for a better model, when you should have said something about my problems with sex and anger and wanting a different body. You don't get it right. You should have told me how much I hate my body and magically want you to change it for another body.

A: [Thinking we had gone over this subject a number of times previously, I responded] When we agree completely, you feel I care. It's difficult when I say something you don't agree with and when our thoughts aren't perfectly in line, then you feel angry with me.

S: No, that's not right. I'm angry with you for other things. I'm breaking links—that's what I'm doing.

A: You think I should think about you in exactly your way.

S: No. I'm not going to speak to you … [She was silent for a time.] I hate you, but not completely or else I wouldn't talk to you at all.

She went on to speak more about the meaning of her dream in terms of her tendency to get inflamed—the angry red car—and how the man in the garage tried to give her a white car in exchange that had excessive miles on it. In the garage she saw a bookshelf with books that had articles about the "authentic self". Then her sister came in with a car with a little pouch inside and she wanted to have one like hers. In the countertransference I felt sad thinking of her envy of her sister, who had recently had a child, and I put this interpretation to her:

A: Yes, you are the angry red car. You believed psychoanalysis would change you into a new white car and into a sexual person with a little pouch with a baby in it. So far that hasn't happened and the white car does not seem like such a good deal and you feel that analysis and I have turned out to be not much good, old and rusty.

S: Why do you say that to me? That's wrong. I told you, the dream has nothing to do with what I feel about you. It is a waste of time to come here today and you don't know how difficult it was to get here.

A: When I have a view that is different from yours, you don't take it in and consider it. You believe I should think in your way, and that you know best.

S: You make me furious. I'm not going to speak to you ... [She was then silent until the session ended.]

Her irritable reaction to me in this session was typical of this period of analysis. She began the next session, which was on a Monday, with:

S: I don't know why I'm here. You don't understand me at all. I'm going to find another analyst. I was totally mad over the weekend and it's getting worse ...

A: When I'm not with you on the weekend you feel outraged with me and you lose me as someone who tries to understand you and help you. You feel angry when there is a gap between us and you are reminded that I have a separate life outside here.

S: You don't understand. You don't listen to me. I said I was mad over the weekend and it was terrible, I was terrified. And you don't say anything to help me.

A: You give up your mind, you depend on me to sort everything out and you don't use the understanding we have reached together and your own understanding mind to help you on the weekend.

S: I'm not going to talk to you, you are completely wrong [long angry silence].

A: When you come here you have to put up with me and you aren't at all happy with me.

S: It's your fault I can't talk to you … [pause] You're crazy if you think I'm going to free associate. Why do I feel that connecting with you will kill me? Outside of here I feel normal, OK, but the minute I see you I feel a terrible irritation. You are my problem; I'm fine until I come in here.

A: [I thought of how this contradicted her initial statement about feeling mad on the weekend, not at all normal, but I felt commenting on this would only inflame her further.] You can't bear it that I have a mind of my own and don't always have exactly the same thoughts as you, but instead my own thoughts. You feel allergic to me, as if I want to poison you. You hate the fact that I exist.

S: [She was silent for a long while. Then she said, more thoughtfully] Something happens when I come here wanting to talk. I want to talk to you until I get here and then a huge hatred surges up and the part of me that wants to connect is obliterated. Then I want to destroy our relationship. Only one thing you said last week has stayed with me, something about thinking that I really want to work with you or talk to you and that I hate it when I don't. That was the only thing you said that was right, but you said this along with many other things about my destructiveness, which were all useless. Though it sounds like I think I know best, I don't think you are saying the right things and then I think you don't know what you are doing and you don't understand me.

[Then she added in a self-satisfied way] Of course, you don't know about several dreams that I've had recently that I haven't told you. But I can interpret those myself.

A: When you keep your dreams to yourself and interpret them yourself, you keep them under your own control. Then, you can imagine we think the same and you don't have to consider anything I say here that might be different. You only want to hear your own ideas and your own point of view. Taking in and considering what I have to say threatens you as it means we have separate minds and you hate that.

S: I'm not going to speak to you … [And she was silent until the session ended]

Up to this time, my line of thinking about Sarah had been that her envious rage towards the early mother and projection of this toxic rage into mother's nipple, and consequently into her link with me, made contact between us dangerous and made me into a bad persecutory object. Envy was clearly part of the picture, but as I thought further about her, in the countertransference I did not feel invaded by projections of rage, greed, or spoiling. Sarah's personality had strong features of narcissism but I did not feel her pattern of relating in the transference could be construed as destructive narcissism that gave rise to attempts to destroy the analysis and the analyst (Rosenfeld, 1971). I felt in Sarah a determination to hang on to the analysis as a source of goodness, but on her terms, which also meant obliteration of my interpretations and of me as a separate person. Her objection to me, her fear of connection and being in my presence, I felt was a rejection of otherness and foreign reality outside herself. At times, Sarah said "No" to me in sessions, as if to say, "I can't possibly take anything in," as if she had a milk allergy, an allergy to foreign protein—which was me as a representative of her mother in infancy. I then saw that my task was to inoculate her, little by little, to tolerate togetherness and the reality of our two minds sharing space (Britton, 2013). She was telling me in different ways that the problem was because "I'm there, because I exist", not as a *bad* object but bad because I'm foreign, alien, not her.

* * *

In the next clinical vignette, I will present excerpts from two sessions that illustrate the second type of patient, the hyper-objective or thick-skinned type, who tries so hard to avoid intersubjective contact.

George

Lacking containment in his early life, George had developed intellectual defences to protect himself from his emotions, including any inner sense of need or distress, and his take on life was entirely rational; this included his choice of career, which was in an intellectual field. His history was chequered with failed attempts to make relationships with women. He sought analysis because of an uneasiness in the presence of both men and women, and an awareness that he was without emotional responses.

Initially hyper-manic, jumping from subject to subject, his internal world was fragmented, his thoughts racing round. He was anxious and mistrustful of the analysis, but as we worked through his mistrust of me in the transference, he began to refer to analysis as a safe harbour, though I felt it was a depersonalised one.

The following is material from a session in the fifth year of analysis, just before a break in which George was due to travel abroad on business and to see his mother.

[George abbreviated as G. Analyst abbreviated as A.]

G: As I become aware this trip is coming up, it has alerted me to the number of people I have to see. I'm loath to meet up with these people; it feels too difficult. My thoughts are tied here. It's always hectic going away, but even more this time.

A: You'll miss me.

G: I'm disturbed about not being able to remember the work we do here when I'm outside the sessions. I tried to think about this last night and today but something always interrupts me. I couldn't remember anything we said yesterday—wait, an image comes—the scary big brother figure that's always there, and no escaping it.

A: There's a part of you, that scary big brother inside, who interrupts and stops you from linking up with me. While you are away I'll be here watching over your sessions, remembering them, keeping them safe for you.

G: [In his typical manner, he did not respond in a direct way to the comment I made.] The big brother figure can have different meanings; yesterday it was my father. I saw L [an old girlfriend] on Saturday. There was an odd tension between us. I want to keep the door open to my friendship with her, even though it is unpleasant. There are so few people I can talk to who share my various ideas. Things feel difficult when I'm with her, when I want more.

A: While you are away you want me to keep the door open for you. I'm the analyst you need to talk to, from whom you want more, yet this makes you feel uncomfortable and odd here.

G: I'm worried about the expectation of me to remember outside here what we do—the slithery ideas that are elusive in normal life. I feel I'm letting the process down. I should be able to instantly understand what you say and access the insights. If you were to give me an exam on what we've said [he laughs] I wouldn't pass it. I thought

I would intuit everything you say and then it all would happen by itself.

A: It is difficult to let my thoughts penetrate you, to keep them inside.

G: I just had a powerful thought about something from last week I do remember—about R [his often-estranged relative]. We started to have a row and what you said helped me to deal with him more sympathetically. I know I'm lacking emotions but I'm more emotional with R than anyone.

A: [I thought at this point that his memory of having taken in something from me was connected with my interpretation about penetration. Then he went on to say:]

G: There's a high current with K [his would-be partner], like there's an electrical fence between us. I manhandle it out of the way, which is effective in some ways, but it's always there. I bristle when she is around. The electrical fence—it is also here.

A: You keep a barrier or fence between us so we don't get too close.

G: It's real, visceral, like with the men I'll be meeting for the university project—even walking around is dangerous, landmines everywhere.

A: Feeling your attachment to me and that you will miss me feels dangerous. Any emotion toward me feels like a land mine.

G: I try to take away what you say and brandish it in the darkness, but it's as though I get it from the library, not as if any emotion is involved. When I'm with my mother too there's a lack of emotion between us. I don't generally feel emotions. I'm in control of myself. While I'm away I will be alone with the fear I had as a child lying in bed listening to the wind making a strange sound.

A: Without me to contain the scary feelings you had as a child, I think you are afraid of missing your sessions and needing me while you're away.

G: Yes, you're right.

A: [I felt this was a moment of contact.]

G: [Suddenly, sitting up and surprising me, looking distressed; it was five minutes before the end of the session.] I had a cup of bad coffee earlier that has upset my stomach. What time is it? I need to go out, sorry. [Jumping up, he left his jacket and briefcase in the room. On returning he said:] I suddenly felt my bladder bursting; I had to pee.

A: We were speaking of feelings around being away next week and I wonder if you felt upset about missing your sessions and wanted to get rid of the feelings by peeing them out, disconnecting from me.

G: I feel uncomfortable about having any emotions relating to here—it's unseemly or awkward. I like to keep everything that happens here in a dry and intellectual place.

A year later, George was less anxious and was feeling depressed. His paranoid anxieties had been defrayed to some degree, and his oedipal fear and guilt had been worked with consistently, yet he kept a distance and I felt the allergic response to me was hardly improved. I reflected on the grim expectations and lack of pleasure he had in life and relationships, but instead of taking up in the transference the frightening things he expected from me, his many anxieties that I had interpreted in so many various ways in the long analysis, I found myself making normative comments. The following is from a session in the sixth year:

G: I've come to realise, I have no sense of pleasure or joy about anything, except maybe music. It came to my attention today, when I was writing a document at work, that I have no interest in the work I do. My attitude toward you and the work here has improved. I'm not intimidated any more; a key point of fear has been broken down. But there's nothing pleasant in my life. it's as if I walk with a limp. I have a familiar sense of sadness.

A: You don't allow yourself to have pleasure in being here or anywhere.

G: Yes, but I'm not really in a huge despond. I'm distant. I have a malaise, like being in the sun for a long time. Like I'm on a beach with a huge wave rising behind me.

A: A beach is a place where you and I could splash and play and enjoy being, but instead you have phantasies that something terrible could happen at any moment. You twist everything into horror.

G: Yes. Last week I thought of what the Brazilian or Argentine police do to children—they put insects under their eyelids. My emotions feed on misfortunes and the horrors of other people.

A: You don't allow yourself to have ordinary human emotions, simple human feelings of two people, you and me, just being here together. Instead you imagine horrors between people.

G: This has come up before. I'm reluctant to take part in the world. I don't know where I am.

A: You don't feel here, not completely present here with me.

G: I think of a prison, a room, and I don't know how to get out.

THE OTHER AS ALIEN: PSYCHIC ATOPIA

A: You can walk out any time but you feel I keep you here. It's harder even to be *in* here, to be here with me, to share this space and be here.

Later on in the session he spoke of feeling more relaxed with me and that he considered the work we did to be important. Nonetheless, I felt acutely the distance he kept from me and how impersonal he kept our relationship.

G: I look forward to the sessions sometimes, but I put obstacles between us. Just had a funny image, strange, like I'm behind a berm or ridge but there's an army tank behind me.

A: When you feel a little closer to me you feel unsafe, as if it's scary to connect with me and you put an obstacle, a berm, between us, but then you feel danger closing in from behind, as if you can't escape.

G: I know I create this idea of a barrier. It's a ridiculous situation, but I don't know how to deal with it; the fear I have here isn't really gone.

A: You are afraid of me. It's hard for you to be here as yourself, as a person in a relationship with me, another person, in a situation where we speak to each other about ordinary things and connect. I think you feel the need to create extraordinary things to tell me, to keep us excited, to keep yourself stirred up.

G: I paint a picture of myself and how anxious I feel. It's insecurity when I'm with others. It's almost as though I want to stay at home, in the kitchen, and not go out and meet anyone. I'm the small child left on the train platform; that's the icon of my interior world.

A: Yes, there is a lonely scared child in you that wants to be in the kitchen with me. Instead you make this space into a train platform, a place where you come and go all alone, keeping everything impersonal, keeping a distance from me, not making a place here like a home where you and I are together and you can feel safe and cared for.

In this session one can see how threatening it was for George to let me in and to be close enough to allow sustained emotional links. Given that he had anxiety from various sources, it was difficult to distinguish whether this was atopia or a primal fear of intrusion. But even when he felt safer with me through the analytic process and could allow some dependency on me as a good enough object, he made a barrier between us that blocked introjects so that an instinctive negative response to emotional contact appeared to be operative.

Discussion

In examining and comparing the material from these two apparently quite different patients, first let us notice their similarities: it is plain they both experienced lack of containment early in life and had not internalised a good maternal object. Both were "difficult to contain" in analysis and found it difficult to make contact and take in goodness from the analyst; an impaired capacity for introjection limited their ability to take in and integrate what analysis was offering. However, little by little they were more able to take in interpretations from me, and over the years of treatment they both improved in terms of levels of anxiety, resilience, and ego strength; they functioned much better in life and got better jobs. And they could allow more emotional closeness to others in their lives.

In spite of their similarities, there were differences in presentation: Sarah strove for oneness and George kept a distance. I propose that both experienced hatred of their object, as if otherness was an alien psychic reality that would harm them, instigating a negative psychic response. With neither patient did I feel there was projective identification as a defence, no indication of primitive splitting, disturbing projections, fragmentation, or fear of dissolution of the ego, as Rey or Klein described in borderline personalities.

Regarding instinctual urges, both patients I have discussed were cut off from their sexuality. Although both were aggressive, omnipotent, and pushed away attempts on my part to approach and connect emotionally, their patterns in relation to aggression were different: Sarah screamed as a baby, constituting aggressive attack, and became thin-skinned and unstable, attacking the analyst, while George turned inwards, hiding and barricading his vulnerability, becoming schizoid and paranoid. Both had aversion to contact and refused the projective and introjective processes that are constantly at work in ordinary relationships to another, yet over time their analyses both ended with a better capacity for tolerating "twoness" and sharing space; they ended with less fear of being penetrated into their deepest and most private space.

In the next chapter, the question of intimacy will be expanded into an exploration of sexuality as it appears in psychoanalysis.

CHAPTER SEVEN

Sexuality in psychoanalysis

Since sexuality has been more openly and publicly expressed in society as a whole from the latter third of the twentieth century, psychoanalytic papers, books, and clinical presentations on the subject of sex and sexuality, paradoxically, have appeared less frequently. Is this coincidental, a sign that sexuality has come out of repression and that patients no longer present sexual difficulties, an indication that individuals no longer have to be ashamed or guilty about their sexual needs in a more permissive society? Or have there been changes occurring in the theory and practice of psychoanalysis that have diminished the role of sexuality and of instinct theory altogether, the ideas on which Freud had based his theoretical edifice and the origin of symptoms? There have indeed been theoretical advances and shifts—most obviously around the development of object relations theory, attachment theory, narcissism, and Bion's notable contribution of theories of thinking, and these new models might appear to have gained in status and influence over Freud's psychosexual model of the mind and of the sexual aetiology of the neuroses. Since Freud's time, in the psychoanalytic literature as well as in psychiatry, patient diagnosis has trended away from the classical neuroses, hysteria, obsessional neurosis, and so on, and towards the various personality disorders:

narcissistic, borderline, unstable, bipolar, avoidant, perverse. However, in my clinical experience, in the area of sexuality there continues to be, as there has always been, malaise and the same inhibitions, dysfunctions, and dissatisfactions as ever. In our consulting rooms, we continue to see problems around frigidity, impotence, or the fusion of sexuality with aggression or masochism.

The apparent de-sexualisation of psychoanalysis led to exasperation in some Freudian circles. Throwing down the gauntlet in 1995, André Green presented a paper to the Anna Freud Centre in London on Freud's birthday, provocatively titled "Has sexuality anything to do with psychoanalysis?". He stated that sexuality had been marginalised and not given its due importance, and called for a restoration of the roles of adult genitality and the Oedipus complex in psychopathology. Green laid the responsibility for the lapse of focus on sexual conflict at the door of Klein and the extensive growth of Kleinian theory. He believed that the modern tendency to think of patients as babies prevented a clear view of sexual pathology and the meaning and function of adult sexuality. Green charged that Klein's focus on the relationship of the infant to the breast in psychoanalytic theorising emphasised the pre-genital and as a consequence of this, sexuality had been cast out from its rightful place at the centre of psychoanalytic thinking.

Green was firm in standing with Freud in the belief that the unconscious is rooted in sexuality and destructiveness, and that our analysis of patients inevitably leads to these elements as we go below the tip of the iceberg. As for the changes in the patient population towards fewer classical neurotics and more disordered personalities, Green expressed the view that personality disorders are defensive in nature, and hidden at their core are sexual and genital conflicts and fixations involving frustration, disappointment, jealousy and envy, and worse: tormenting anxiety and guilt, terror of being taken over or losing the self, and fearful avoidance of object love due to latent unconscious phantasies of conflict and violence. Reaching these phantasies is the issue, and in his argument, Green was essentially asking for more pleasure and Eros in psychoanalytic thinking.

Seemingly in response to Green's challenge, in 2003 the Anna Freud Centre titled their Twenty-Fifth International Scientific Colloquium "Has sex left psychoanalysis?". At this colloquium, Birksted-Breen (2003) presented a paper on sexuality in the consulting room that stated that there is no doubt that sexuality dominates the psychoanalytic encounter—it is just a matter of whether it is silent sexuality or noisy sexuality. Ruth Stein's (2003) paper at this same conference, linking up with the theories of Laplanche, suggested a re-mystification of sexuality, recognising its subversive and ecstatic nature that necessarily transgresses boundaries. Later, Fonagy (2008) weighed into the debate, claiming that neither drive theory nor object relations theory adequately describe the difficulties around sexuality that are regularly presented in the consulting room. He attributed sexuality's power to dysregulate the individual to the mother's lack of mirroring sexual arousal in the infant and child. Fonagy's research showed that whenever a child appeared to be sexually aroused or masturbating, the mother looked away, thus creating an alien presence of a strange absence in the mental space of the child. Fonagy argued that this lack of mirroring is overcome in the adolescent when his or her sexual excitement is found through the other, discovered when it is mirrored by the other, and thus, through empathy, sexuality is found to be acceptable. In this way, according to Fonagy, the sexual self is recognised in the other, whereby sexuality can be internalised and normalised, integrating the ideas of Stein and Laplanche with attachment theory.

Following the movement towards what seemed to be a re-sexualisation of psychoanalysis, the European Psychoanalytical Federation held a conference on "Passion, Love, and Sexuality in Psychoanalysis" in 2010. Many books and articles followed, as psychoanalysis appeared to be embarked on a second wave of sexual theorising. The papers from the EPF conference brought in the centrality of infant sexuality and the pleasure principle as fundamental to psychic life and the importance of libido, Eros, and desire in the life of the adult. Many British psychoanalysts had absorbed French theories of sexuality and Laplanche's (1989) notion of the mother's unconscious seduction of the infant, which imbues sexuality with a sense of the mystery of enigmatic erotic messages from the mother.

This re-fortification of psychosexual theory is all very well, though, in my experience, sexuality and the Oedipus complex have never been marginalised in British psychoanalysis, and, in my view, Green was misguided in this. Following Freud's unequivocal statement that the Oedipus complex is "the nuclear complex of the neuroses" (1909d, in his footnote on p. 204), British analysis, in my observation, has maintained a sensitivity to oedipal issues, and to their offspring, triangularity, as central to the structure of the mind, particularly in Kleinian theory

(Rusbridger, 2004). By the same token, the erotic transference has by no means disappeared, as can be verified in clinical discussions and ethics committees. Furthermore, in the long analyses of patients with personality disorders, sexual conflicts are regularly found at their core, as I will discuss in the clinical vignettes presented below.

Klein's view of sexuality was seen through the lens of the Oedipus complex, and she wrote about the Oedipus complex all her life, with a particular emphasis on the primal scene. In the Kleinian literature, analysing and relinquishing oedipal love is a central feature of the psychoanalytic task, linked to the depressive position and the acceptance of reality (Rusbridger, 2004). Without doubt, intense love and entanglement with a parent can constitute an unconscious fixation interfering with adult relationships. Oedipal anxieties and jealousies can be revived throughout life whenever three-ness occurs in phantasy or in real relationships, and particularly in the analytic situation.

The child, excluded from the parent's love relationship, may elaborate unconscious phantasies around parental intercourse, powered by feelings of being deprived in relation to the particularly loved parent, a sense of being left out of the excitement and the action. In Kleinian theory, the phantasy of parental intercourse is inborn in a rudimentary form and later filled in by experience, and, in the pathological situation, the primal scene can be the focus of the infant's intense feelings of jealousy, hatred, guilt, love, fear, aggressive attacks, and other complex projections. For Bion, the primal scene is an innate template, which he names a "preconception", and if it is not distorted or destroyed by later experience or projections, and if the parents' intercourse can be accepted, then making links and the capacity to think are enabled generally, the notion that verbal intercourse is based on the pattern or template of sexual intercourse. In the case of violent primal scene phantasies, sexuality can be distorted, creating personality disturbances and thinking disorders.

Freud linked sexual anxiety and the Oedipus complex with hysteria, a diagnostic category no longer in use in psychiatry but alive in the Kleinian literature. For example, there is Britton's (1999) often-quoted remark about disturbances in sexuality: the hysteric seeks to "mount the stage" and join in the primal scene. In an example of the role of the primal scene in understanding complex hysterical symptoms, a paper by Sodré (2015) discussed a patient whose severe hysterical symptoms were traced to an unconscious phantasy of identification with the erotic link between the parents, an excited introjection of and identification with the "perpetual orgy" (p. 221) of the primal scene. This identification, together with the patient's desire to participate in the parents' sexual coupling and her anxiety about this, is an extreme form of oedipal illusion. Sodré believed that the identification with the parents' sexual activity had powerful consequences for the patient's whole mental life, and therefore for the nature of her object relations—this, she said, constituted the neurosis.

From my perspective, the centrality of sexual conflict in the aetiology of the neuroses has altered little since Freud's time. In the four case examples that follow, I will illustrate analytic work with the erotic transference and the Oedipus complex that shows how anxiety and conflict about sexuality were at the root of neurotic, psychotic, and borderline disturbances.

The erotic transference

The intimacy of the analytic situation, with its invitation to use the couch and the freedom to free associate about fantasies and dreams, can arouse intense desire in a patient. Perhaps due to the situation of abstinence and non-gratification, stirred by infant sexuality, by enigmatic sexual messages from the mother, or by oedipal desires, however the erotic transference develops, it represents an irresistible, mysterious, often terrifying but beckoning transgressive feeling of sexual excitement, whether silently or noisily.

If an erotic transference is manifest and the analyst is afraid to speak of the patient's sexual feelings, afraid that he will inflame them, he is on dangerous ground. When the erotic transference, or countertransference for that matter, is unacknowledged and avoided, the pressure of instinctual desire may push for expression and acting out. There is a strong tendency to want to ignore erotic feelings, to push them away and hope they will go away. About the difficulties of analysing the erotic transference, Britton wrote:

> Some analysts seem nervous of making explicit their understanding of their patient's illusional [erotic oedipal] transference for fear of stimulating it. But silence on the topic is much more likely to confirm the patient's wishful belief that there is an unspoken secret between them. Others do not want to expose their patient to the

realization that their erotic belief is an illusion for fear of hurting
them or humiliating and enraging them. (2013, p. 7)

Rosenberg (2011) writes of the difficulty of interpreting erotic feelings in
the transference: "the analyst is wary of interpreting the erotic for fear
of articulating what might, in fact, turn out to be her own sexuality"
(p. 60). She recognises the importance of the erotic transference in freeing repressed sexuality: "As repression becomes eroded by the analytic
process, sexuality is once more in search of an object" (p. 52). This can
be seen in the case of John, as follows.

John

When sexual material begins to appear in analysis, signalling that
sexuality is emerging from repression to find a place in the patient's life,
there is opportunity for its integration. This occurred with my patient
John, who was in a lengthy four-times-per-week analysis. He was the
only child of battling parents who divorced when he was five. He was
passed back and forth between his parents, and then sent away to school
as they found new partners, leaving him feeling lost, rejected, and
unwanted. John was timid and afraid of women during his adolescence
and early adulthood, but in his mid-twenties, wanting the security of a
relationship, he tried going out with several strong, dominant women
who bullied him but also looked after him and made him feel safe. The
sexual side of these relationships was either awkward and unsatisfactory, or absent. The women had all the power, and he felt emasculated
and victimised, unable to be sexually potent.

After settling into analysis, and working through some of his
unhappy past and his many grievances and traumas, sexual material
began to come into the sessions. John told me of an incident when he
was riding his bike to work and suddenly became aware of thoughts
about having sex with a woman who was a workmate; then he crashed
and fell off his bike. I responded, "Hmm, a workmate". He went on
to talk of other things. Then, in another incident, he told me that as
he was going into the underground, he fell down the stairs, and could
remember that just before falling he had been fantasising about sex
with an exciting woman. I interpreted that I thought the woman represented me and linked this fantasy with the fantasy of the workmate he
had mentioned earlier before crashing his bike. Further, I interpreted

that sexual desire in his mind was associated with violent crashes and with pain instead of pleasure, as if sexual fantasies were forbidden and needed to be punished. I spoke to him of his having formed an unconscious link between sexuality and violence in his mind, as if he believed his battling parents' sexual intercourse was violent and destructive, and I said that he had internalised this as his idea of what sex was bound to be like with a woman. Soon after this, John told me at the beginning of a session that he had a fantasy that I had been upstairs in bed with my partner before he came in, and I interpreted that he was curious about my sex life. He acknowledged that this was so. A few sessions later, he reported that he had a dream the night before about having sex with a woman, who, he said, might have been me. I interpreted directly that he had erotic feelings towards me, to which he answered yes, but did not elaborate. Analysis proceeded without further mention of sex, and after a few weeks John told me that he had started a relationship with a woman and was having passionate, fulfilling sex for the first time in his life.

Mr C

In a very different example, another patient of mine in a long analysis, Mr C, was the only child of a busy mother and absent father. He was left alone with his fantasies for much of his childhood. Lacking containment for his emotions, Mr C had developed an intellectual and narcissistic defensive organisation to protect himself from emotional disturbance, any inner sense of longing, need, or distress. His take on life was confined to the rational, including his choice of career in an intellectual field. His history was chequered with failed attempts to make relationships with women. He sought analysis because of a deep feeling of uneasiness and anxiety in the presence of both men and women, and an awareness that he was without ordinary emotional responses.

In the initial period of the analysis, Mr C was highly anxious in my presence, and I began to sense the strength of the unconscious phantasies that held sway over him. As we explored what these might be, it manifested that he was afraid that our close proximity meant that I wanted sexual contact with him and wanted to draw him into a sexual relationship, which felt very scary. When I interpreted how anxious he was about this, and that he both feared and wished I would seduce him, his anxiety diminished noticeably. Over time in the analytic process, these fears reappeared in different versions, and putting his fears into words meant that he became less anxious overall in the transference and able to speak more freely of his feelings and fantasies. Due to his experience of the analytic relationship as consisting of fantasies, emotions, and words that passed between us, and that actions did not follow, he began to feel more secure inside and outside the sessions.

But his fear of seduction was not only in the here-and-now of the session. Mr C was repelled and frightened by any thought of sexual union, which was displayed when he spoke with disgust of "the beast with two backs", a primal scene image of the combined parents stuck together in a perpetual, aggressive sexual orgy that felt terrifying. It was an image that also contained his own projected aggression. This introject is similar to the way in which Sodré's (2015) patient internalised the parental sexual act, resulting in severe hysterical symptoms.

I interpreted that he experienced me as the beast, that I was perceived by him to be not a singular person but, instead, two people engaged in constant sexual intercourse, excluding and upsetting him. It was clear he was relieved by these interpretations of his phantasies. Mr C illustrated vividly to me how the primal scene, because of the excessive and powerful nature of repressed sexuality, was at the core of his psychotic anxiety. With deep insecurities brought about by an unprotected and deprived childhood, my patient sexualised all his relationships so that even speaking to me or to anyone felt like sexual intercourse, which I regularly interpreted.

It transpired that Mr C's sexual anxiety surfaced in a new variation—a sudden frightening fantasy that an angry man might abruptly enter the consulting room and threaten him. He said on the first occasion, "I just had a strange image of a man bursting into the room, who is very angry". After this happened two or three times, I realised that this was an oedipal fantasy, and I interpreted this figure as a representation of my partner, whom Mr C believed was jealous and enraged by his close relationship with me. I added how this linked with fear of the return of his absent father, about whom he fantasied a great deal as a child. He remembered a childhood friend, the two of them were the only children in his class who mysteriously were without a father. The friend's father was away in prison, and he recalled wondering whether that was where his father was, too. I said that he believed as a child that his father would be angry about his closeness to his mother and return from prison to attack him. Clearly, the absence of Mr C's father during his childhood prevented a normal Oedipus complex from developing, and from being lived and worked through.

Interpretations about his sexual fear and oedipal guilt continued for some time and allowed sufficient working through so that his external relationships with both men and women became less fraught, and he began to feel attracted to women and to be able to have friendly relationships and to feel closer to them.

Elsa

Interpreting the erotic transference requires careful timing and dosage. As Rosenberg noted, "the wrong interpretation—or the wrong moment—can change the level of the analyst's utterance from metaphor to seduction" (2011, p. 61). A male psychotherapist whom I supervised in the NHS had a borderline patient, Elsa, a young woman who had a history of cutting her body, arms, and thighs whenever internal tension reached unbearable levels. Borderline patients are well known for their strong emotional response to the therapy relationship, their intense transferences, both positive and negative, and their inability to bear separation. Initially, the treatment centred on the patient's negativity and suspicion of the therapist. Interpretations of the negative transference led to a more positive transference and, as this took hold, the woman would go into the lavatory outside the consulting room after the sessions and cut herself, reporting her actions to the therapist in the next session. In supervision, I discussed with the therapist how this behaviour might be communicating that, when the therapy sessions were experienced as good or helpful for Elsa, it meant that separation at the end of the session was infuriating and unbearable, which she expressed by cutting herself. Elsa was angry and wanted to "cut off" the therapist, in retaliation for his cutting *her* off when the session came to an end. This the therapist was able to take up and interpret.

After working for several months on her rage about many past injustices, many of which could be interpreted in the transference, as well as her anger around separation between sessions and over breaks, just before the summer holiday Elsa brought to a session two cupcakes decorated with white icing, each with a cherry on top, and presented these to the therapist. Aware of the meaning of this gift, the symbolic offering of her breasts in transference love, the therapist was afraid to interpret the erotic transference directly, given that it was the last session before the long summer break and such an interpretation, he felt, would be likely to be too disturbing. Instead, he remarked only that she was giving him a gift so that he would remember her and think about her over the break. When Elsa returned after the break, the negative transference had returned and increased, which I attributed to her feeling that her symbolic gift of her breasts had been refused. Stormy times followed, with Elsa's angry denigration of the therapist, walking out of sessions and threatening to quit the treatment; the therapist struggled to contain her aggression and make sense of it as disappointment and anger with him and the therapy, and the painful feeling of abandonment by him over the break. Then the patient brought a dream that exposed her intense anxiety around sex and relationships. In the dream, she was with her therapist in a ruined castle with crumbling walls. They were kissing and it was lovely. Then she went away and took part in various activities, after which she returned to the castle and panicked as she began to bleed profusely with streams of menstrual blood.

It seemed the dream indicated the state of the patient's fragile self as a crumbling castle, not strong enough to contain her anxiety and fears around sexuality. Her defences against erotic feelings had crumbled: there was a lovely kiss, but this turned into terror and a traumatic fear of bleeding to death. Surrendering to intimacy and love meant in Elsa's unconscious phantasy that her lifeblood would pour out of her, reiterating the cuts she had inflicted on her body as a simulacrum to a bleeding vagina. The appearance of her transference love and its dire consequences in the dream image made possible the formation of mental representations and symbols that could be worked with, enabling words and thoughts to be ascribed to her terrifying unconscious phantasies around sex, femininity, and the primal scene, which were worked with over time. Although this was partially helpful in reducing anxiety and self-harm, this patient's inability in the long run to let go of her love for the therapist, and to accept that "I couldn't take you home", meant that the rage of a woman scorned led to an abrupt premature ending to the therapy.

Polly

The last example I will give is Polly, a woman in her thirties who was in analysis for six years, three times per week. On the surface, and before she married, she appeared to be uninhibited in regard to sex, both with her previous boyfriend and with her fiancé. However, after her marriage, she stopped having sex with her husband, and struggled with deep inhibitions and conflicts around sexuality together with the wish for a child.

After a long period of not dreaming, she told me a series of four dreams:

> I'm feeling much better today. I know I was angry and complained about D [her husband] last week, going on and on; I was having a rant. I've had four dreams the last four days in a row; I can remember only parts, just snippets, not all of them. [She went on to tell me the dreams, one after another, all in one go.]

> In the first dream, I was with D and another couple in their lounge; we were playing music and dancing around, having fun. I pulled up my skirt and was surprised I had on a thong. D said, "Those aren't proper knickers". I looked and realised only a tiny bit of my vagina was covered. Then I woke up.

> I was with another woman with long dark hair, about my age, I link her with an aggressive, envious woman who I know; we were chatting and there was a hint of the erotic. She said a friend was coming and the sexual tension heightened. Then a strange person came in, a fat man dressed in drag as a woman, with a white wig. He was disgusting; I felt sorry for him. He was sad and deflated and started talking about work.

> The following night, I dreamed about the wonderful Julian, that's my gorgeous male friend at work; others were there, a woman; it was a working day in the office. Though I knew he had a girlfriend, I went into a room with him; it felt warm and nice. He wanted me to cuddle him. I felt fond of him. We came out of the room, and I felt afraid others might see us and I would get in trouble. He said something about his ex-girlfriend, I said, "Ex?" and he said, "Yes, ex". Then I woke up.

> In the dream I had last night, I was kissing a friend's boyfriend. They were about to get married and I was thinking he was a good kisser. I guess that means I want sex, doesn't it? I was sick this morning and D asked me if it was morning sickness. We had decided a while ago not to use birth control and to try for a baby. Yes, in my dream about my vagina and knickers, having an opening there feels very uncomfortable. That's it, really, my unease about

sex. As an adolescent I got it all confused. Like I was defenceless against an angry penis, left with a vulnerable vagina. My body feels aroused and wants sex but my brain won't let me. I'm afraid that will always be my default position, yet I yearn for a baby, I have fantasies about it all the time. But I always want a different man than the one I'm with.

My patient's series of four dreams tracked her shifting position in relation to sexuality and her difficult conflicts and inhibitions around sex. I saw the dreams as representing a series of changes in her phantasy life, what Catalina Bronstein calls "transformations in symbolic forms" that are attempts in the unconscious to resolve conflicts and work through paranoid and depressive anxieties.

In the first dream, Polly felt more relaxed about sexuality in the context of a pleasant evening with friends, dancing around the room, but in the end of the dream she felt vulnerable and unprotected in relation to masculinity. This led in the second dream to homoerotic feelings in relation to a woman as perhaps a safer option; however, as if her unconscious was warning her that there would be the risk of envious aggression with a woman, she shifted excitedly towards the masculine, and a man appeared who turned out to be terribly disappointing, a degraded figure in drag towards whom she felt disgust and contempt. Moving away from these images as if rejecting homosexuality and men whose developed (or perhaps undeveloped) feminine side was felt to be ridiculous and unappealing, she turned in the next transformation towards Julian, the idealised, sexy, desirable but unavailable, man in the third dream. Even though she knew that he had a girlfriend, she set up a covert triangular situation, cuddling him, and made him appear tantalisingly single and available. In the fourth dream, she moved more clearly into the triangular oedipal situation, focusing on her friend's fiancé, the good kisser, kissing him in symbolic intercourse. This situation, I felt, enabled her to feel safer in connection with her sexual desire when both a man and a woman were involved, two figures representing parents. The fiancé of her friend was spoken for, off limits, which in my view demonstrated unresolved oedipal desires and the wish to take the man away from the woman.

These dreams and associations to them opened up rich material that could be taken up as the analysis continued: her inhibitions and fears of sex, which she felt to be sadistic penetration; her contempt for men; her homoerotic urges, which she rejected; and her central oedipal dilemma, wanting to be in a sexual couple but afraid, putting herself into the place of a child in the oedipal triangle, always wanting a different man representing the unavailable father and, ultimately, afraid to take the mother's place and inhabit the role of the oedipal couple in relation to her own man, and become a mother herself with a child of her own. This would have been a travesty, given Polly's history; in phantasy, this would mean she had been responsible for the elimination of her mother, who left the family when she was little, the tragedy of her life. In the transference, too, letting me in at times felt like an invasion, a harmful penetration, as we worked with her anxieties.

Discussion

All of my four patients, John, Mr C, Elsa, and Polly, I believe, illustrate Green's notion that personality disorders are formed as a defence against deep unconscious sexual and aggressive anxieties. For each of them, I could discern a violent, dangerous primal scene phantasy that was at the root of their neurotic anxieties, a phantasy of the intercourse between battling, murderous parents that was essentially psychotic. And each had different configurations of the Oedipus complex.

John responded directly to my interpretations of crashing his bike and falling down the stairs as violence fused with sexuality, and the erotic transference carried him into disinhibition of his libido as he felt his sexuality was accepted by the analyst. His personality defence was as a weak, dependent man, but the course of his analysis showed him to be quite the opposite, in his career and in his relationships, as he found his potency.

Mr C had built an intellectual/narcissistic defensive personality organisation to deal with his terror of sexual relationships, as they invoked the horrific conscious primal scene fantasy of "the beast with two backs", the perpetual orgy of the primal scene. This was complicated by an oedipal phantasy of a punitive father who, on release from prison, would come back and seek him out for punishment because of his desire for his mother, which appeared in the consulting room as a fear my husband would be angry with him for his closeness to me. Mr C became much less afraid of men and women as the analysis proceeded, but continued to find emotions difficult.

Elsa's borderline personality disorder was an attempt to contain her powerful overwhelming fear of sexuality and rage towards the desirable object, involving cutting and self-harm. Sexual partnership for her meant bleeding to death. However, in the safety of the transference, her passion was unleashed, as was her fury at unrequited love.

Polly had a primal scene phantasy of battling parents that appeared to have eliminated her mother, who left the family when she was young. It was moving to experience with Polly her struggles to resolve her anxiety around sexuality and her conflicted wish for a child.

Conclusion

Green's claim that psychoanalysis had been de-sexualised appeared to have stirred up an international response, and a more overt interest in sexuality seems to have followed. I found his claims to be stimulating in thinking about patients' defensive organisations and what they are designed to be defensive against, and I agree with him, although I doubt that sex has ever left psychoanalysis. Certainly, sex never left French psychoanalysis, fortified by the influence of Laplanche's (1989, 1997) theories of maternal seduction and the mother's enigmatic messages, transmitted as phantasies, which, according to his view, establishes the infant's sexual unconscious.

The erotic transference is always a potentiality in the consulting room in its noisy form—in fantasies, dreams, or associations—and ubiquitous in its silent form—in the deep unconscious primal connection to the analyst, underpinned by infant sexuality. Erotic love is the prototype of pleasure, inhibition its banishment. Analysis, in my view, must have as its ultimate aim the search for and link with libidinal desire, the freedom to pursue love and passion, whether in its sublimated form or as sexual pleasure.

Patients, generally speaking, do not speak of sex unless there is a problem, but many patients seek analysis and therapy for help with sexual problems. For a person to allow him- or herself to have the powerful, disrupting experience of falling in love and having sex is a trial to individual identity: self-boundaries are lost as the self is propelled into oneness with the other in the experience of passionate love, an experience that can engender a terror of losing the self completely and of not being able to find it again. Love relations may involve acute anxieties around separation and loss of the object. As McDougall (1995) put it, because sexuality ruptures the normal envelope of body and mind, and breaches the boundaries of self and other, it is traumatic. For all of us, falling in love is a bit like a borderline state: loss of control and inability to regulate one's emotions in the overpowering encounter with otherness. If this can be negotiated, the self can be found in a new light with an expanded identity, but possibly one that includes unwanted elements such as intense emotions of jealousy, possessiveness, and fear of loss.

The next chapter will be given over to an obstruction in analysis that disallows the person to use analysis to feel better, be better, to find an identity, and to enjoy the pleasures of life. Freud conceptualised this phenomenon as the "negative therapeutic reaction".

CHAPTER EIGHT

Negative therapeutic reaction re-examined

On the face of it, patients come to analysis in order to feel better, and this is their conscious intention. It is all the more surprising and distressing when treatment exposes contrary trends in their personalities that work against their manifest aim. Freud first wrote of "negative reactions" in 1918 in relation to the Wolf Man, who contradicted the good effects of his analysis by bringing back a symptom that had been cleared up. It was typical of Freud to examine difficulties posed by his new treatment as they presented themselves and he continued to reflect on these until the end of his life. It is still important today for clinicians to re-examine theories and techniques, particularly in the region of setbacks and impediments that can stand in the way of analytic progress. The concept of the negative therapeutic reaction (NTR), relatively neglected in recent times, will be discussed in this chapter along with clinical vignettes that aim to cast light on obstacles to psychoanalytic development.

Freud defines the NTR in his 1923 paper, *The Ego and the Id*, which sets out his structural theory of the mind, by saying:

> Every partial solution that ought to result, and in other people does result, in an improvement or a temporary suspension of symptoms

produces in them for the time being an exacerbation of their illness; they get worse during the treatment instead of getting better. They exhibit what is known as a "negative therapeutic reaction". There is no doubt that there is something in these people that sets itself against their recovery, and its approach is dreaded as though it were a danger. (Freud, 1923b, p. 49)

In the first place, Freud attributed the NTR to unconscious guilt, but, he said, instead of feeling guilty, the patient feels ill. He continues:

In the end we come to see that we are dealing with what may be called a "moral" factor, a sense of guilt, which is finding its satisfaction in the illness and refuses to give up the punishment of suffering. (Ibid.)

Freud proposed that these patients have ego ideals that place strict demands upon them to be morally unassailable and faultless. These demands are difficult enough to meet in life, but prove an impossible feat when the patient's belief is that he is guilty of wrongdoing that cannot be forgiven. Freud goes on to discuss how the analyst can approach the sense of guilt, felt by the patient to be unbearable, by carefully unmasking its unconscious repressed roots and gradually changing it into a conscious sense of guilt that can be borne and perhaps worked through. Vignette 1 shows an early NTR in ascendance.

Vignette 1: Anna

In a case that I supervised, the patient was a young woman of thirty-three, whom I shall call Anna. Her mother had been hospitalised for postnatal depression when she was born, and as Anna grew older, her mother was often ill, staying in bed for long periods of psychiatric treatment. Anna had two brothers aged nine and ten when she was born. During Anna's childhood, her mother frequently told her that she hadn't wanted to get pregnant again and that her birth was unwanted, and the reason her mother was ill and so unhappy. Their relationship had never felt close or warm for the patient. She turned to her father for friendliness and companionship, and as time went on, they shared many interests and she grew to love him greatly until he died in her early twenties. Anna blamed her mother for his early death. Unable to form a good relationship with a man or to advance in her work, spending her weekends in bed, alone and depressed, she started four-times-weekly analysis.

She established from the beginning a good working relationship with the analyst, and she began to experience the containing function of the analytic process, becoming more active and enjoying her weekends. She was feeling better; however, it was clear that she avoided speaking of her "dark thoughts", at which she would only hint: her hatred of her mother, her suicidal impulses, her badness, and her self-loathing, all of which had haunted her all her life. She tried to keep these thoughts out of the analysis in spite of the analyst's attempts to bring them in.

After about a year of treatment, which marked a period of feeling helped, she decided to apply for a better job, for which she clearly had the ability, and planned to prepare the job application and then have a week's holiday with friends, stating her determination to have a good time. Returning to her sessions after the break, it transpired that she had not put in the job application, had not gone on holiday, and had spent her week off at home, alone in bed in a dark depression.

Anna tried to describe how desperate and bad she felt: "I think about death, about being ill, about things going wrong. I ruin things. I wish I would stop. I have no faith. I think everything is going to go bad and that I am fated. I am fated for everything to go wrong and to be bad, so why even try. I keep thinking bad thoughts about what you think of me. I know you will say that this space is for me but I don't think that. I don't feel bad about not trying to help myself. I feel bad about the fact that you could be seeing somebody else who would benefit so much more than me and I feel so guilty and bad."

In supervision we viewed this as a negative therapeutic reaction to having been understood and helped by analysis and for a time feeling better, and we worked on how the analyst could show Anna that withdrawing to bed and depriving herself of a good holiday and a better job was due to the "something in her" that would not allow her to have good things in her life. This "something" we formulated as her guilt about ruining her mother's life and, as a consequence, bringing about the early death of her father. As the analyst became able to link up these ideas for Anna, she began to have some insight into how deeply guilty she felt, having been convinced by her mother that she was the cause of her unhappiness and depression. She was able to identify feelings of guilt about having been born, and then more guilt about her alliance with her father, an oedipal triumph over her mother, that led her to believe that she did not deserve to have a good life, a better one than her ill mother.

The concept of NTR

The concept of NTR has often been misused, applied as a general catch-all phrase to denote obstinate resistance to change met with in treatment or to write off failed analyses, by saying that the patient's wish to remain ill or to gain from suffering is stronger than the benefits that analysis could offer. However, I maintain that it is a useful concept present in every analysis and can be understood as analysable resistance. Owing to the progressive and regressive nature of psychic growth, the frequent movements forwards and backwards, and movements between paranoid and depressive anxiety, NTRs are bound to occur, and their severity is dependent on the amount of unconscious guilt and superego strength that resides in the patient. If these states can be analysed as they happen, as an inherent part of the analytic process, they can be understood and dealt with so that over the longer term the possibility of good results from the treatment can be maximised.

Freud pointed out that the NTR shows itself by "a negative attitude towards the physician and clinging to the gain from illness" (Freud, 1923b, p. 49). He outlined in his earlier discussions of symptom formation that symptoms represent a primary gain from illness by solving a libidinal conflict, and a secondary gain that provides the practical advantages of enabling the person to receive special care and consideration or being able to influence or manipulate others. Thus, at a most fundamental level, the patient can refuse to improve because doing so constitutes losing the secondary gain—the special status of being ill—and, most particularly, were he to be well, losing the analyst by the ending of the analysis.

Thus, secondary gain is closely linked with separation anxiety. To a degree, this occurs in every treatment and particularly in the final stages. But with patients who are at the more disturbed end of the spectrum and who have difficulties in containment of their primitive anxieties or in their capacity to think, separation problems are very much in the forefront. These are the patients who form adhesive or symbiotic relationships with the analyst; for them, separation takes on catastrophic proportions, so that any advance in the work or expression of satisfaction with progress on the part of the analyst will bring about panic at an unconscious level, as it signals a feared imminent or eventual end of the treatment. This is demonstrated by immediately feeling worse, suffering a return of the symptom or the development of a new one, as if the patient is saying, "I can't possibly be better; see how bad things really are. I need to continue treatment."

A number of writers have linked NTR with the masochistic personality, a chronic determination to suffer or an erotised addiction to punishment. These are patients who consistently deprive themselves of pleasure, who don't reach their potential at work or allow themselves to have satisfactory relationships, who neglect themselves and deny their needs. Modell (1965) speaks of them as patients who do not feel they have "a right to a life of their own". Asch (1976) thinks this is due to identification with a self-sacrificing masochistic mother, an early maternal object that the patient cannot relinquish. Similarly, Fairbairn (1952, p. 117) writes of masochism as a tie to childhood bad objects, whereby the badness is taken into the self in order to deal with it there, resulting in a masochistic character. Jean Begoin (1998) points out that masochistic patients often present as victims, maintaining a suffering that is not masochism per se, as suggested by Freud, but persecution that is projected outside into external reality, blaming others, resulting in a victim mentality. Suffering or victimhood may have been established in the personality as part of their identity, a condition that will need to be addressed by the analytic work. The next patient I will discuss used victimhood in a particular way.

Vignette 2: Ben

Ben was thirty years old when he began analysis with me, beginning at three then moving to four times per week. He had been in analysis for five years at the time of writing. Throughout his life Ben had systematically sabotaged his opportunities, including his education. He came into analysis when he found that he actually wanted to make a success in a field in which he was doing a degree, as he was finding the field exciting and full of promise and did not want to do a demolition job as he had in the past. An only child, Ben's parents split up when he was four, and he was agonised and bereft when his father moved out of the family home and a stepfather moved in, and later, terribly upset and jealous when father married a woman who bullied him and with whom

Ben, on his visits, was in frequent conflict. In his twenties he, too, chose women who bullied him and he felt very much the victim. He would go to his parents to complain, crying and desperate about his unhappiness with his current partner and his life situation, getting them to tell him what to do but never following their advice. He married one of the bullying women, against their wishes. It became quite clear from early on that Ben believed that if he were happy and successful he would lose the attention of his parents. This was a pattern that had begun in childhood when his misery at home and at school demonstrated to everyone that he was a "problem child" who needed the attention of both his parents, hoping to bring them together over his difficulties, something of which he was vaguely conscious at the time. Ben felt ignored and pushed aside by his parents, angry that they were getting on with their own lives, blaming them for his misery and craving their attention. He got it by having problems, bidding for their sympathy, and making them feel very guilty.

In the transference, I was repeatedly made to feel sorry for him and he tried his best to get me to tell him what to do. As we began to see his unconscious patterns, it became clear that Ben was getting his revenge on his parents by messing up his life, tormenting them with his failures. He would often torment me by failing to come to sessions, telephoning to cancel two minutes before his early morning session, showing me how it felt to be unwanted and pushed aside, excluded from his parents' relationships, as he had felt in his childhood. Each new piece of insight brought some improvement in his life—a good deal of success in his work, better sexual functioning, less anger, and a bit more optimism— but he would soon return to misery again, blaming and punishing his parents. For this patient getting better meant losing his objects, which was confounded with a determination to punish them, with concomitant guilt about this. He told me that he didn't want to get better since it would mean losing me, which also meant, I said to him, losing opportunities to punish me as a parental representative with his masochism and sadism.

As our work went on, Ben had more experiences of contact and insight into his internal world, one in which he felt hopeless, a world in which everyone had let him down—a bad mother, father, wife, and analyst— where there was nothing of value to be had from anyone, where he was unable to love, and the only satisfaction available to him was the hidden, triumphant revenge on his objects through his own victimhood.

As he became aware of this, he was appalled and depressed by this view of himself; he began to struggle with his negativity and to gain some sense that until he could feel empathy for his objects and let go of the sadistic/masochistic link with them, releasing his guilt, he would continue his repetitive, destructive patterns. To accept separateness and the sadness of loss in the depressive position was an ongoing struggle.

Narcissism and depressive anxiety in NTR

Not so theoretically far removed from the masochistic personality are certain narcissistic problems as the source of NTRs. Much has been written about narcissism as a psychic situation in which there is a withdrawal of investment from external objects and a cathexis of internal objects, particularly of the ego or self. Describing a way in which narcissistic patients present in treatment, Abraham in his 1919 paper discussed what he termed "narcissistic character resistance". Abraham thought these patients tended to get stuck in their analyses, due to an inability to receive what is given by the analyst. They mask their failure to free associate by speaking of their problems in a friendly, superficial way, carefully arranging their material, speaking only well of themselves, and forgetting that they are in analysis to treat their neurosis. They don't develop a true positive transference and any true negative transference is hidden. When the analyst makes interpretations that point out anything about them that might be construed as critical or unpleasant, they react with hurt, anger, or humiliation; they have the characteristics of what we now call "thin-skinned narcissists" (Rosenfeld, 1987, p. 274). In Abraham's experience, even a long analysis does not succeed very often in penetrating narcissistic character resistances; the patients exhibit what he termed "anal omnipotence" and are unconsciously defiant and competitive with the analyst, in constant revolt against the father, wanting to do everything by themselves or telling the analyst how things should be done.

Rosenfeld (1971) thought of setbacks in analysis as due to "The narcissistic omnipotent delusional part of the patient which feels threatened by progress and insight" (p. 81), an attack on the sane part of the ego by the narcissistic destructive self. In the NTR the psychotic part maintains power by preventing interpretations from reaching the needy infant part of the self or preventing the patient from experiencing the benefits of a period of good analytic work.

Studying Abraham's description of the narcissistic resistances, Joan Riviere (1936) wrote that she believed what was operating in Abraham's patients was the NTR, that there was a latent depression within them that was strenuously defended against so that they made their real feelings untouchable, with a consequent failure of introjection of good experiences or of the analyst as a good object.

In discussing the NTR, Riviere (1936) thought of it as a defence against an underlying depressive anxiety that is difficult to reach. Her paper on the NTR is important in that, quite early in the history of psychoanalytic thinking, she extended the theories of Freud, Abraham, and Klein on the subject, and in doing so made a considerable contribution of her own. For Freud it was the severe superego that brought about therapeutic setbacks; for Abraham it was the narcissistic character resistance, with its omnipotence and refusal to accept from others. Putting these together, along with Melanie Klein's work on internal objects, manic defence, and the depressive position, Riviere wrote about an organised system of defence that masks an underlying, unconscious depressive condition in the patient. She vividly describes a situation in which the patient is terrified of encountering this depression and will go to extreme lengths to prevent it happening, believing he would be driven to madness or death.

Riviere wrote movingly about the internal world of these patients in a passage that is often quoted:

> The content of the depressive position is the situation in which all one's loved ones within are dead and destroyed, all goodness is dispersed, lost, in fragments, wasted and scattered to the winds; nothing is left within but utter desolation. Love brings sorrow, and sorrow brings guilt; the intolerable tension mounts, there is no escape, one is utterly alone, there is no one to share or help. Love must die because love is dead. Besides, there would be no one to feed one, and no one whom one could feed, and no food in the world. And more, there would still be magic power in the undying persecutors who can never be exterminated—the ghosts. (Riviere, 1936, p. 313)

This is a picture of an excruciating depressive area in the internal world that encompasses the patient's belief that his internal objects are so damaged or destroyed through his own aggression or neglect that they can never be repaired; he is guilty; there is no goodness in him. There is the conviction that, "my objects are in a terrible state and I am responsible". This is an unconscious region in psychic reality that is split-off and segregated, avoided by the patient; to be put in touch with this depressive area evokes a terror that he fears will overwhelm and destroy him. Thus, psychoanalysis is dangerous if successful. Any change, the patient thinks, would be a change for the worse, so he is determined to keep everything as it is, to protect the status quo. In the patient's experience, he has reached a certain equilibrium that means that, while his life may not offer happiness or success, there is at least an avoidance of catastrophe if he continues as he is. To maintain equilibrium, the patient attempts to exercise a subtle control over the analyst that is often difficult to analyse; he controls the process, choosing the material, sidelining or ignoring the interpretations, manically defending against contact with depressive anxiety. By keeping his inner life still and dead and maintaining omnipotent manic control, he can avoid the terrible truth that he has not loved his objects enough and kept them well, and that loved ones in his internal world are also the object of hatred, scorn, cruelty, and murderousness.

Even though sadistic phantasies are found in everyone, in some the depressive position is stronger and their belief in goodness has little foothold, perhaps linked to early trauma. In spite of a conscious wish to get better, for these patients it is difficult to allow the analyst to help them by letting him in and working with their depressive beliefs and fears. The patient feels that by becoming better and happier he will abandon his objects, leaving them behind.

Riviere's key contribution was to notice that although outwardly the patient may appear self-centred, egotistical, and lack real feeling for others, inwardly it is the opposite: he embodies conscious selfishness and unconscious altruism. The patient believes that were he to recognise the damage he has done, he would have to expend all of life's energy making amends, repairing his objects. As this situation is untenable, his internal reality and the depressive position must be defended against at all costs. The next case I will discuss illustrates many features of this dilemma and shows how guilt and suffering can become a part of an identity.

Vignette 3: Catia

A woman patient, whom I shall call Catia, began analysis at the age of thirty-three. Having had an early marriage that turned into a disaster, she met and married her second husband, a man who adored her, who was kindness itself, who helped her in many ways, and who was also financially well-off. They had a baby together who was nine months old when she began treatment, three then four times a week. As a couple they had begun talking to a child psychologist about how to be better parents, and the psychologist suggested individual treatment for Catia.

At assessment she told me she suffered from chronic feelings of being bad and worthless, and at the same time she felt no one else was any better, and she felt contempt and dislike for everyone. She was unhappy in her marriage and anxious about almost everything. Although intelligent and functioning more or less adequately in a chaotic, manic way, it was apparent that her inner world was wildly turbulent, with conflicting emotions and circular thinking that were a source of maddening distress to her.

Catia immediately took to the couch and found relief in speaking of the complicated thoughts and feelings that troubled her. She spoke very quickly, everything tumbling out, often inserting irrelevant details, clauses that twisted and turned, and often going off on tangents. Beginning to listen to herself speak of things she had never told anyone before was a source of amazement for her, and it was clear she had never had a space within herself for self-reflection. My early work with her was around interpreting how hard it was for her to stay in one place, to remain with one thought, and not rush on to the next.

She told me a complicated history of being the eldest child, with two younger siblings, of a mother who was overly concerned with how things looked on the surface, and whose marital difficulties involved divorce, disruption, and loss for the children. Her father was alcoholic and volatile, yet Catia remained close to her father until he died when she was an adolescent. As for her mother, she told me: "I adore my mother. We are very close but she drives me crazy."

In the first week after moving from three to four sessions a week, she became extremely disturbed by news broadcasts about the abduction of the British child Madeleine, from a holiday resort in Portugal. She had repetitive, obsessive thoughts about the plight of the child and the parents, weeping uncontrollably for several days. Her distress seemed to be alleviated when I interpreted her upset as stemming from anxiety around the safety of her own daughter and her own childhood terrors, though I wondered at the time whether this signalled an NTR, as she had just increased her sessions from three to four. In seeking more intensive help for herself, it appeared that she felt the increased investment in herself was disinvesting her daughter, leaving the child in danger, which I interpreted. She agreed and told me that she felt guilty whenever she took any time for herself or focused on her needs during the day. She felt too guilty. She either had to be busy or to look busy, particularly when the nanny or cleaner were around. She would have preferred to look after the baby herself, but felt the nanny, who had such a good relationship with the baby, did it better.

A few months later, after finding the analytic work helpful in stabilising her and in organising her mind and her daily life, she went away for what was meant to be a happy weekend with her husband, feeling an improvement in her relationship with him. Then, over the weekend, terrifying thoughts of Madeleine's kidnap, and of another newspaper report of a Burmese woman who sold her child into prostitution for £50, kept coming into her mind, distressing her and spoiling the weekend. After telling me of this, Catia spoke of her guilt and deep sadness about the awful things that go on in the world, saying, "I don't want to get rid of guilt, something bad will happen to me." She told me of her secret fantasies of being alone and free of her family, living out a hedonistic, romantic vision of herself in which she had wild affairs and led a colourful bohemian life; guilt, she thought, kept her from acting this out. Longing for this wild life induced feelings of unworthiness about the privileges she enjoyed with her husband. The recurrent, tormenting images of the abused children spoiled the benefits of the improvements she had made in her state of mind and turned a pleasant weekend into a painful one. She could not acknowledge or enjoy the good things in her life and be grateful for them, since, as she told me, "Being grateful means adding pain to the unfortunate people. How can I be happy when so many others aren't?" A picture similar to Joan Riviere's description of the NTR was becoming visible, which became the focus of the analytic work.

Some time later Catia became pregnant with her second child, a planned pregnancy, and she was delighted. She said that now she had a purpose in life, a reason for being: she was making a baby inside, so she didn't feel so useless. A new child meant that she had a reason for caring for herself, eating well, looking after herself, and that it was OK to smile and be happy: "I'm allowed to look after me when I'm pregnant, because it's looking after my new baby, and I'm pretending it's not to do with me." She was able to soothe her guilt by caring for her internal object in a concrete way in the womb.

I began to see a pattern in her sessions in which she would do some good work on a problem, reaching a point of near resolution, and then undo all of this work. In an example of this, a theme had developed around her difficulty in feeling she was the "lady of the house"; she had a constant feeling of posing, of acting the part, pretending. Then she told me that recently she had been able to ask her cleaning lady to do something, rather than trying to please and placate her as was her usual way, and it was OK. She also remembered she had asked the builders to do something too, that she was feeling more comfortable in her position and was able to ask for help and get things done at home. She moved on to speak of provoking a row with her husband that brought back unhappy feelings from her past. Those awful feelings were a part of her, and without them she didn't know who she was, she told me; they were part of her identity. Then she circled back again to say that she felt a fake in having a nice home, a ring, a nice husband, as if she had to compulsively undo whatever feeling of accomplishment or contentment she had reached. When I showed her this pattern—that after reaching a point where she could recognise a change for the better, she undid the good work and moved back into the bad feeling—she told me that when she allowed herself to feel good, she got anxious, as if leaving behind bad feelings made her feel afraid.

Several of the following week's sessions consisted of this theme, how she held on to the "dark side of her", linking to past experiences with her seriously dysfunctional, violent first husband and her disturbed father, saying, "I can't let go of these things; they feel a big part of me. If I do, I'll have no identity." A particular area of guilt kept resurfacing around her father's death, which she felt she hadn't mourned properly. At the time, she was happily enjoying a carefree adolescence, drinking with friends, going out on the town; she remembered feeling a little sad, but not very sad, about his death. She was her father's favourite child and gained that position over her siblings by being perfectly well-behaved in his presence, appeasing and pleasing him, but afterwards suffering guilt when she got favours and presents from him that her siblings went without. Then she confessed to me that she couldn't bear that her husband took time to satisfy his own needs, even though they were mostly for the good of the family, while she couldn't do that for herself. It made her angry when he took a long time to chop the vegetables, which he enjoyed, or to send emails, and she felt particularly angry about a trip abroad he was planning (a rare occasion, for they were seldom parted) to attend a stag party for an old friend, and for having pleasures that she could not allow herself. She became aware that seeing him happy made her angry and envious, and then terribly guilty: "Of course I really want him to be happy—he is so generous and good." On Friday she felt in a better state of mind after speaking of these things, and said that she wanted to leave behind the anger and guilt, and the feeling she was constantly plagued by: that she was not doing enough, being enough, or giving enough.

By Monday, however, she came to the session feeling awful, suffering from severe morning sickness and feeling guilty about her sister and a friend she had been with over the weekend who were both unhappy: "I feel guilty when they are unhappy because when they are unhappy they want more from me. I have more than they do, and I feel guilty about that, so I give too much of myself and then I feel resentful and exhausted." She described this "giving too much" in her relationships at great length, a peculiar way in which she lived in projective identification with her objects, making strenuous efforts to be the person they needed or wanted at that time, being a different person for each relationship, projecting an image of herself as a wonderful friend, of themselves as also wonderful, just like her, using her prodigious imagination to sort out their problems and paint a glowing picture of the world for them to take away and be happy with. It was clear how entering the minds of others in this way, decorating their interiors with idealised twin images, and being "all things to all people", as she put it, left her out of touch with her own identity and without any real sense of herself. As she told me: "I'm just learning that it's OK not to become the other person when I'm with them, even though that makes me a more boring, less exciting person." The analytic work was helping her to "feel comfortable in her own boots", as she put it, which she complained of never having felt before, through the process of getting in touch with and reflecting on her own experiences, her thoughts, beliefs, and feelings, including guilt and unworthiness.

It was astonishing how little sense Catia had of her own needs. She couldn't imagine having them met, telling me that this was a completely new way of thinking. She said, "Here is a small example, but it's really a big, big deal and typical. My husband wanted orange juice from the shop and asked me if I wanted juice too? Instead of saying

I wanted coffee, which I did, I said OK, I'll have juice. But then I felt resentful and irritated. Like, I can't let myself have what I want and enjoy it. I can't enjoy my marriage. I'm constantly setting myself up to be a martyr." I spoke of how not asking for what she wanted made her feel deprived; then she could play the victim and blame her husband. She said, "As soon as you flag these things up I can see that it doesn't need to be so complicated. I want to have my needs met. But if I ask for what I want and get it, I'll become selfish." I said she feared that being aware of herself, her needs, and having them met meant she would be so selfish that she would only think of herself and neglect others. She responded that it was opening a can of worms, that if she had her needs met everything would fall apart, her husband, the children, the nanny, the household, as if she controlled them through her selflessness and kept everyone going by her martyrdom. I viewed this as manic, magical reparation of the objects she unconsciously attacked in phantasy, the family she wanted to leave so she could have the wild, exciting, free life of her phantasies.

In following sessions, she enumerated many instances of how she spoiled any pleasurable experiences she might have, spoiling pleasure to bring herself down to the level of others, depriving herself of advantages. She began to "diss" all the nice things she possessed, expressing a wish to sell her house and move back into a small ordinary flat with her children or thinking she had married the wrong man. I began to think she might act out impulsively on these wishes. She said, "I can't be grateful for anything. I'm too guilty about all the others in the world who don't have good things." I continued to interpret her guilty belief that unless every unfortunate and unhappy person in the world was made happy and well, she could not allow herself to be well.

Some time later, after an agonising debate with herself that had lasted for several months, Catia sacked the nanny with great difficulty, against her usual impulses to please her, and began to enjoy caring for her baby. Soon after this she wanted to reduce the number of sessions and spoke of not wanting to come, preferring to be at home with the baby, which I interpreted as her wish to sacrifice herself to her family and to neglect her own needs. I also interpreted her anxiety about coming face to face with what was beginning to emerge in her sessions, glimpses of her internal world peopled by terrifying images, scary punks, robbers, and thieves, the "ghosts" of her dead and damaged objects. She told me several dreams in which she was in her childhood home being threatened by vicious punks or frightening men. When she described a childhood dream of a masked thief appearing at the foot of her bed who was stealing the silver and valuables and I interpreted that she was afraid that I would break into her mind and steal her valuable thoughts, she said that made her feel good, as if she had something inside that was valuable, instead of the complete inner badness that she usually felt. She again spoke of the terrifying male figure that as a child she would see at the end of the bed when she awoke at night. I wondered with her whether this appearance had to do with the absence of her father after he left when she was two, a small child longing for a lost father, and so creating his presence at the end of her bed. In the next session she told me that this interpretation had made her feel nice, less scared, thinking of the man as her father. I kept in mind the man as having a more complicated, overdetermined meaning, connected to ongoing work around oedipal anxieties and desires, but principally at this point I felt she was anxious about aggression from internal persecutors and night-time spectres. Then, I began to think that her fears were about propaganda and abduction by an internal gang (Rosenfeld, 1971) that sought to control her and threatened to draw her into destructive activities, selfishness, and self indulgence. I tried to convey to her that, in my view, this linked with her fear that having her needs met would open a can of worms.

As time went on, Catia became more committed to the analysis, as she felt it helped her to negotiate the external world and to be less afraid of her internal world; she was developing an identity, a reflective function, and a mind of her own. Transference interpretations, however, startled and unsettled her; she wanted to keep me as an anonymous, impersonal function rather than a real person. As I persisted in exploring our relationship, what was happening between us, I could sense some positive feelings towards me, in spite of her worry that she had no love in her. In the treatment of NTR patients, Riviere stressed that it is only by reaching the hidden love in the transference and the craving for love under the surface of control that the analysis will advance. Riviere wrote: "… the true analysis of the love and guilt of the depressive anxiety-situation, because they are so deeply buried, is by far the hardest task we meet with." (1936, p. 320). The psychotic phantasy that the patient's love will spoil and destroy their objects means that they evade closeness and deny their need for love, remaining in a state of deprivation.

In the last example, I will discuss Danielle, whose guilt around oedipal rivalry precipitated a period of severe NTR.

Vignette 4: Danielle

A borderline patient of mine in a long analysis, Danielle, was a divorced, forty-five-year-old woman who had trained as a lawyer. Her father had committed suicide in her adolescence and her mother was cold and uncontaining. In our work together, Danielle had revealed a pattern of very difficult or ruined relationships, high emotionality, and a dispersed and erratic sense of self, which had improved in many ways over time. For several weeks before the Christmas break in the sixth year of treatment, she had been feeling more stable and calm, was doing better at work, and felt positively toward me in the transference as a helpful person, not so much as a persecuting, withholding mother. A week after the break she suddenly became miserable and was unable to sleep, expressing feelings about the emptiness of her life, her love and longing for her lost father with whom she had been so involved in an especially close relationship before he died, one that excluded her distant mother. She felt furious thinking about the Christmas break, which no doubt I had spent with my husband in a happy, warm relationship, while she had been alone and wretched. She complained bitterly that I had given her the desire for a partner again but that now it was too late. With a ferocious determination to pull down everything we had constructed over six years, Danielle entered a sustained, destructive NTR that lasted for two months, a vengeful attack that threatened to destroy the analysis. She withdrew from me, would not speak for sessions at a time, halting the analytic process. She told me a dream in which there was an earthquake that reduced her flat to rubble, starting a fire; in spite of her efforts to salvage her possessions, all was lost, a terrible catastrophe. This mirrored the way in which she was reducing the analysis to rubble, leaving her with a sense of having nothing. More dreams of chaos and madness followed, and, projecting her psychic pain into her stomach, what had been a mild, intermittent gastric condition became a crippling stomach ache that prevented her from going to work. She was attacking her mind as well as her body, her capacity to think, and the self-structures she had developed in analysis. Launching fierce attacks on our work and on me, she told me that I was no good, that I hadn't helped, that I didn't understand her, and she demanded that I do more for her.

Slowly the destructive tantrum subsided; its end was announced by a dream about a dangerous flame that was reduced to a flicker. In the next session after the dream, on a Monday, Danielle spoke of wanting to bring me a gift and missing me over the weekend. The storm was over, at least for a time. My work with this dangerous NTR was to speak of her intense anger towards me, and her fear that I wouldn't be able to weather her hostility and destructiveness. I tried to show her how she couldn't allow herself to feel well, as she had been before the break, and to continue to benefit from the analytic work she and I had accomplished, due to rage about loss, loneliness, rivalry with her analyst, and oedipal guilt in relation to her father.

Discussion

In examining the four cases I have discussed in this chapter, one can see similarities in regard to the experience of benefits gained from the psychoanalytic work, which is then followed by setbacks, with guilt as the common factor. However, differences can also be discerned. In my view, what we call the NTR can have a number of different origins in different patients without diminishing the value of the concept, if we see an NTR as a phenomenon that is expressed in different ways.

For Anna, it was a straightforward example of unconscious guilt that was not allowing the patient to progress in her life or in her analysis. She felt guilty about hating her mother and shame about having been born, believing she was the cause of her mother's misery and depression.

In the case of Ben, his victimhood and failure were gratifying in terms of punishing his parents and his analyst; at the same time, his unacknowledged, hidden guilt was projected into his objects to make them feel guilty. Ben's self-sabotage, masochism, and sadism were actively keeping him miserable and dependent; he had no confidence in being loved as a healthy person, only as someone who needed to be looked after, and he searched for interminable care from his parents and from the analysis.

In the third vignette, it could be seen that Catia had formed a narcissistic defensive organisation comprising a manic, omnipotent belief that she could repair and restore all her damaged objects (and all those suffering in the world) through being what others needed, sacrificing her own needs and well-being. Her defensive organisation protected against psychotic depressive anxiety, persistent guilt and self-blame, and a sense of inner badness, so that she left the care of her child to a nanny and could not enjoy her marriage or her privileged life. As long as she had very little of her own—a miserable first marriage, a humble lifestyle—her life felt bearable. Good fortune, a good marriage, and wished-for children were not felt to be deserved. As with Freud's patients, "those wrecked by success" (Freud, 1914c), Catia's sense of guilt prevented enjoyment of her life.

In the fourth example, Danielle, consumed by oedipal love for her father and oedipal jealousy of my relationship with my partner over the break, entered a destructive period in her analysis, driven by intense oedipal rivalry and rage. She found it unbearable to think I had a partner when she was without one and she raged against this, punishing both herself and me. Oedipal guilt, I believe, was the mainspring of her NTR, along with persecutory guilt about anger and destructiveness.

Even with these different origins and motives for reversing the progress of the treatment, I maintain that these four examples primarily illustrate NTR and not differing concepts. The characteristic element linking them is unconscious guilt, even though the source and object-relationship pattern was different in each case: hatred of mother, victimhood and sadomasochistic links to objects, psychotic-depressive guilt, and oedipal rivalry. This view of NTR distinguishes it from a commonly held notion that reversing progress in analysis springs from envy, or is a manifestation of the negative transference in which aggression or perversion hold sway over love and reparation. In an example of this, Karen Horney described the NTR as the situation when a "good interpretation" brings relief and improvement, and then a negative reaction sets in. Horney believed good interpretations stimulate envy of the analyst and trigger aggressive attacks on the analyst and the analysis (Horney, 2007, p. 30). This is similar to Klein's view of the envious attack on the good breast that supplies help and relief, indicating that the patient cannot bear to depend on a source of goodness that is outside the self, compelled to reassert omnipotent self-sufficiency. Although the importance of envy cannot be denied, overusing it to interpret a range of negative reactions would be erroneous, I believe, as it would be to attribute these reactions to an aggressive or perverse character.

It would also be wrong to give the impression that all negative reactions to treatment can be turned around. However, expecting them to occur regularly as part of the analytic work will help us to be prepared for helping the patient to dislodge the belief that punishment and self-sacrifice to assuage guilt are the only recourse. Freud noted that patients do not readily believe us when we tell them about their "unconscious sense of guilt" or their "need for punishment" (Freud, 1924c, p. 166), and they may hold on to illness and suffering in order to satisfy their conscience. Even when the patient has a conscious awareness of guilt, we may find ourselves up against, and will need to counter, the misguided notion that atonement can only be made through personal failure or self-sacrifice, or that any possibility of working through, or reparation of self or object, must inevitably fail.

As analysts, how do we talk to patients about their bleak and unforgiving internal worlds? Freud wrote in *Civilization and its Discontents* (1930a), "… we are very often obliged, for therapeutic purposes, to oppose the super-ego, and we endeavour to lower its demands" (p. 143). How we do this involves the application of the art of psychoanalysis, to show the patient how self-blaming, unforgiving and cruel he is towards himself.

In the next chapter, moving away from the severe superego, I present the work of the French artist Odilon Redon as an example of the artist's creative dialogue with the unconscious as a means to produce symbolic representation. The chapter will discuss the psychoanalytic view of symbolism and the way symbols are formed as they appear in dreams.

CHAPTER NINE

Symbol formation and dreams: the art of Odilon Redon

During the same time that Freud and Jung were opening the doors to the unconscious through dream interpretation, taming its anxieties and demons, and exploring symbolism and unconscious phantasies, the French artist Odilon Redon (1840–1916) was painting strange pictures with images springing to life from his imagination, insisting on their right as creations of the mind to exist in and for themselves. Redon worked contemporaneously with the Impressionists but rejected their preoccupation with the exterior world in favour of the interior world of fantasies, dream-like images and apparitions. He created symbolic creatures and visual oxymorons that emerged from inner darkness, as if from the heart of unconscious symbol-making.

The impact of Redon's work is a profound sense of disturbance, awe, and mystery. The space created by his canvasses is ambiguous and otherworldly. His work evokes feelings of elation and mystical union and, at the same time, reminds us how human suffering can edge towards psychotic states. His own emotionally deprived childhood fed his vivid imagination (Hobbs, 1977, p. 10), often becoming a visual language of madness, yet simultaneously, in Redon there is a conviction that redemption is possible through aesthetic experience.

Redon's interior discourse with the imagination is presented as something fascinating in itself, as if Redon urges us to examine the oddness of his images and not shun or fear them; he inspires us to appreciate them for their intrinsic value as natural children of a fervid nature. I think there is a parallel to be found in the work of the psychoanalyst, who may be called upon to examine strange or terrifying dream images, to trace their possible symbolic meanings and to examine their place in the patient's psychic space.

Like Blake who preceded him, Redon was subject to hallucinatory experiences and visions: "… I have sometimes seen in the sky awesome, half-formed heads and bodies emerging from dusky blackness, fallen angels" (Werner, 1969, p. vii). His pictures not only give life to these strange creatures, but appear to suggest symbolic meanings. Just as Jung called symbols "the best possible expression of a relatively unknown fact" and Levi-Strauss described them as "bricolage", images gathered from the odds and ends of experience, Redon joins together unlikely images that suggest new, ambiguous meanings, bringing together, for example, the worms and amoebas of the earth with celestial faces of desire. The chimera, the smiling spider, the cactus man, the cyclops, etc., form visual oxymorons, the linking of opposites. The images verge on the pre-symbolic, which adds to the sense of mystery and disquiet.

For Redon, anxieties and phantoms appear as doors to adventure, the fantastic behind the ordinary, the mystery behind the appearance: a plant blossoms with a face; a balloon becomes an eye. Intriguing and unsettling, the real is linked with the unreal in improbable existences that are original, and that inspire and urge towards the unknown, the integrative.

Unlike many artists, Redon was quite conscious of his intention. He writes, "I speak to those who yield, quietly and without the assistance of sterile explanations, to the secret and mysterious laws of the sensibility of the heart." And, "Suggestive art can provide nothing without recourse to the mysterious game of the shadows … it … is the radiation of various plastic elements which are combined and brought together with a view to stimulating reveries … and … encouraging thought" (Druick, 1994, p. 202).

Redon was inspired by the engravings of Dürer and Rembrandt, and his early work echoes theirs. Rembrandt's method of taking the material world and imbuing it with a spiritual dimension was especially influential to the young Redon. He became fascinated by botany and zoology and his work took on organic elements. He studied zoology books and copied bone structures found in natural history museums. In his early work, he preferred black and white tones, stating, "Black is the most essential of all colours … It does not waken the eye and awakens no sensuality. It is an agent of the spirit far more than the fine colour of the palette … a power drawn from deep sources which acts directly upon the mind" (Werner, 1969, p. x).

Redon said of his lithographs, "My lithographs should be like music, something uncircumscribed that everyone can feel and understand in his own way, a theme upon which everyone embroiders his own dream" (Druick, 1994, p. 179). He produced seven books of lithographs between 1879 and 1897. To the first, *In the Dream* (1879), the critical response was recoil: "bizarre" said the critics, and "a nightmare carried over into art" (Werner, 1969, p. vii). Redon's answer to his critics was to declare his belief in, "A right that has been lost and which we must reconquer: the right to fantasy" (ibid., p. viii). Then came further series' of lithographs—*To Edgar Allan Poe* (1882), *Night* (1886), *The Origins* (1883), and

Homage to Goya (1885)—and as his reputation grew, he illustrated texts by Flaubert, *The Temptation of Saint Anthony* (1888), and Baudelaire, *The Flowers of Evil* (1890). The titles he gave his prints were often small literary productions in themselves, prose poems with equivocal meanings but always suggestive, for example, "When life was awakening in the depth of obscure matter", "The chimera looked at everything with terror", "Death: It is I who make you serious". Falling into the abyss was a recurring theme, for example, a centurion falling from his horse-drawn chariot into a dark abstract space, or "The fallen angel", whose face of profound melancholy, sporting heavy wooden wings, represents perhaps, like Ariel, the spirit's reluctant link with the earth. Put together, his titles formed stories of man's evolution as he arose from materiality to spirit.

Only in the 1880s, when Redon was forty, did he begin to be known in Paris as an artist to be reckoned with. He was highly regarded by his fellow artists for his profound interior visions, and at sixty he was awarded the Légion d' Honneur. He was taken up by the literary avant-garde in France, the Symbolists, as part of a movement that transformed French intellectual life. The Symbolists were searching for a new way to represent reality and to become free from the dominance of Realism and Romantic decadence that they thought had held the nineteenth-century in its grip. The Symbolists were interested in the mystery of language and its power to allude and suggest associations through ambiguity, using image and symbol as catalysts. Their influence was felt widely into the twentieth century, offering British writers such as Forster, T. S. Eliot, and Woolf, as well as the Magical Realists, new ways to conjure the world (Hobbs, 1977, p. 24; Werner, 1969, p. ix).

In the misunderstandings surrounding Redon, he found himself labelled as a foremost Decadent before the turn of the century. René Huyghe, the distinguished art critic and conservator of paintings at the Louvre, defended Redon, pointing out misunderstandings: that his art was neither decadent, literary, nor modernist, in the sense of subjective, abstract combinations that flee the real. His was, stated Huyghe, the synthetic art of the symbol and its companion, the imagination, as the basis of all meaning. His images were a correspondence between external reality and subjective internal states, whereby an emotional experience is re-invoked by the symbol. As such, Redon prepared the way for Surrealism. (Hauptman, 1964).

One might ask to what degree the images invoked by Redon were authentically from the spontaneous unconscious, the true creator of meaning. In *Hysteria*, a celebrated play by Terry Johnson (1993), Freud is visited by Salvador Dalí, who asks him to comment on one of his paintings. Freud says he finds in Dalí's Surrealist work only conscious contrivance, while in the still lives or landscapes of painters like Cézanne, he sees a constant play of the creative unconscious. In the play, Dalí is so influenced by the opinion of the inventor of psychoanalysis that he responds, "This means the death of Surrealism." The same criticism—conscious contrivance—might be made of Magritte or Ernst or Redon as well, a too-conscious (or self-conscious) representation of the imaginative play of the unconscious. However, their value in terms of their symbolic meaning speaks for itself.

At the end of his life, the pessimism that had always been with Redon gave way to a confidence in life and a great joy. He gave up black-and-white and took up colour, producing exuberant flower paintings. The flower became his ultimate symbol for life and the expression of the spirit.

The rediscovery of the mystical symbolism of Redon and an apprecia-tion of him as a key figure in twentieth-century art appeared perhaps as a response to a current spiritual hunger to find inner sources of what Redon called "the radiance which possesses the soul", and as an anti-dote to our present-day functional commodification and materialistic preoccupations. Redon's images ultimately defy verbal description, and operate by signs and hints that stimulate the imagination and excite at a level beneath articulation and analysis, gratifying our unconscious longing for something not seen in our mirror images or our "selfies", but a link to a universe beyond our own egos.

Symbol formation in psychoanalysis

In psychoanalytic theory, as in art, the imagination is in constant play, producing images and symbols shaped by the unconscious at the crossroads of body and mind, the place where mental entities emerge from the material reality of body experience. According to dictionar-ies and common usage, a symbol is an image representing something else, usually charged with significance and meaning to convey the importance of the original entity. Though much of our conscious mind is concerned with the everyday, unconscious symbols in our internal world represent our deepest longings, desires, and need for safety, and give shape to our activities and thereby our attempts to live meaningful lives.

From birth, the infant's experiences in relation to the mother, her breasts and body, are the crucible of symbol formation. Melanie Klein (1930) has given a coherent account of how symbols are created: the infant is born with rudimentary primitive symbols or pictograms that are filled in as experience accumulates to form unconscious phantasies. As the infant has good and bad experiences with feeding and care, these evolve and form good and bad internal objects which are used symbolically; the infant goes on to form phantasies of the parents' relationship, the father's penis, the primal scene, and the Oedipus complex.

Klein saw phantasy as active and ubiquitous in the child, expressing itself in all the child's activities. She found children's play to be highly symbolic and expressive of symptoms and pathology, and she used play as a technique in child analysis. She wrote extensively of the symbolic representation in the child's mind of good objects that are internalised to enable internal security and stability.

As the baby develops, Klein shows how the child naturally turns to toys as symbolic substitutions for mother and her love when she is unavailable or when anxieties accumulate around oral and anal aggressive attacks towards the absent breast:

> The child puts his love and hate, his conflicts, his satisfactions and his longing into the creation of these symbols, internal and external, which become part of his world. The drive to create symbols is so strong because even the most loving mother cannot satisfy the infant's powerful emotional needs. (Klein, 1963a, p. 299)

Klein was particularly interested in the child's anxiety in relation to the mother's body, and wrote of periods of infant sadism and aggression that disturbed the relationship with the mother, the phantasy of devouring the breast and possessing the contents of mother's body, or of using faeces and urine to attack the mother. Anxiety about aggression and fear of retaliation force the infant to develop new symbolic representations, choosing toys, dolls, balls, etc., to love and to hate, bringing about an interest in new objects, endowing them with symbolic meaning, leading to ego growth and a relationship to the outside world. Thus, Klein saw symbol formation as essential to the development of the ego:

> ... not only does symbolism come to be the foundation of all phantasy and sublimation, but more than that, it is the basis of the subject's relation to the outside world and to reality in general. (Klein, 1930, p. 221)

For Klein, the development of symbolism is a crucial element in the capacity for object relationships. When there is a disturbance of the earliest object relationships, symbolic function is disturbed, which in turn prevents the formation of further object relationships.

The study of symbol formation in psychoanalysis is a large subject and only some key contributions will be mentioned here. Jones (1916) formulated the central thesis based on Freudian theory: the symbol is formed when a desire for something or someone is in conflict with circumstances and must be given up; both the desire and the object of desire are repressed and pushed into the unconscious as representations, following Freud's idea that when the object is lost it is recreated in the ego. But Jones did not see the importance of symbols for sublimation, whereby in the unconscious, the symbolic representation seeks substitutes, displacing affect and interest into new, different but similar activities and objects out there in the world. In this way, the primitive desires are sublimated. Sublimation is the basic and necessary activity for all mental development, including the acquisition of language, thinking and the capacity to endow the world with meaning. It was Klein who elaborated precisely how this process is accomplished through projective identification.

Jung (1969) also gave importance to symbol-making, positing unconscious complexes as universal symbols that drew mental energy to them. Winnicott (1965, p. 145) had his own take on symbol formation, beginning with the hungry infant's hallucinations of the mother's breast. He thought when the breast then appears, the infant imagines it was summoned by his own omnipotence; this encourages the breast to be internalised as a reliable, useful symbol. Further symbol formation takes place through transitional experience and play with mother as the child develops. Segal (1957) contributed the important distinction between the true symbol and the symbolic equation, a primitive, concrete version of the object. Bion (1962, p. 90) conceptualised the container and the contained as symbols for various levels of psychic functioning. The container/contained is a flexible symbol representing the baby's mouth/mother's nipple, mother/infant, the vagina/penis, the mind and its contents, the analyst and the patient, etc. It is an abstract formula for the place that receives projections and the content of the projections, which are the crucial symbols for underlying psychic order. Bion (1992) named the symbol-making process "alpha-function" and saw it as the inherent process for the creation of meaning, as distinct from "beta-elements", which are raw and unprocessed emotional matter, unassimilated and without meaning. In his intriguing Grid, which tracked the evolution of thought, Bion suggested that meaning and thinking originate in the mind as basic processes and then move to more complex sophisticated constructions, from intransigent beta-elements, to alpha-elements that create dream thoughts, leading to preconceptions, conceptions, and concepts, usable in the thinking process and in forming abstract systems of thought.

In psychoanalytic treatment, unconscious symbolic meaning is found in the interactions between the analyst and patient: through free associations, interpretations, dreams, enactments, gestures, slips of the tongue, bodily sensations, and many other subtle or obvious ways. For the individual in treatment, symbolic meaning is drawn from that individual's internal life, history, and experience; known symbols can signify objects consistently and regularly, while new symbols arise from the unconscious that introduce new ideas, emotional experiences, and understanding. Symbols tend to represent what is most vital and preoccupying: family relations, people close to us, sex, birth, life, and death. Symbol formation needs a container for its conception, originally the mother's body and the baby's mind; in analysis, it is often the dream and the analyst's mind.

Dreams

Just as symbols play an important part in psychic reality, so do dreams. Freud presented his controversial theory that dreams have an important psychological function in *The Interpretation of Dreams* (1900a), where he discussed the way in which dreaming is central to symbol formation and mental representation, translating pre-symbolic sensual and somatic experience into images with symbolic content, which Freud later conceptualised as thing-presentations or word-presentations. Dreams are able to slip by or push through the censor that guards the border between the conscious and the unconscious and, when interpreted by Freud's associative technique, their meaning can be unveiled to reveal the deep structure of the mind.

Dreams are felt by many to be the fountainhead of creativity. The unconscious is poetic and symbolic. An early analyst, Ella Sharp (1937) wrote eloquently of the way in which dreams employ metaphor, simile, and symbol to express mental life. She spoke of the dream as "poetic diction" in the language of the unconscious, and dream interpretation as translating poetry into prose. Often the unconscious speaks in metaphor, a concise, sometimes ambiguous verbal expression or figure of speech that reveals meaning and psychic structure. Marian Milner (1979) was another analyst who was deeply interested in dreams, which she saw as a creative attempt to symbolise life experience; she described the analytic session as the frame that surrounds a painting, the content of which is created jointly by the analyst and the patient. Khan (1976) stressed the importance of dreaming in "actualising the self", creating identity. Padel (1987) emphasised that dreams involve the real psychic work of altering symbolic meanings in unconscious phantasy, bringing about changes in the personality. Freud's original idea of the dream as wish-fulfilment, functioning to preserve sleep, has been expanded in regard to the anxiety dream or nightmare, which was elaborated by Ferenczi (1931) in suggesting that dreams serve to rework and attempt to master psychic trauma. Night terrors or chaos monsters can be called forth in dreams by disturbing experiences or stress. Behind the censor or split-off from consciousness may be emotions of guilt, anxiety, shame, or sorrow that we don't want to know about but which, without due attention, can adversely affect our present-day life. In the poetics of the dream there is displacement, where one idea may stand for another; for example, an animal may stand for one's child self, or figures such as a chairman, president, or pope for one's father. In displacement activity, tending the garden can represent cultivating friendships or organising one's life; redecorating or refurbishing the home may represent being in analysis. Ideas are condensed in the dream, where a number of ideas may be grouped into one symbol; for example, a dream of climbing a mountain may stand for one's ambition, pride, or a notion of oneself as a hero. The residue of childhood magical thinking may be at work in dream life.

Segal (1981) differentiated between symbolic dreams and dreams of events in ordinary life. She drew attention to the use of dreams to evacuate, as distinct from communicative dreams. As Kleinian theory developed, dreams came to be thought of as the nearest derivative to unconscious phantasy and as the central mental process for making symbols and creating meaning. According to Meltzer (1981, 1983) dreams are the internal space "where meaning is generated" and dream interpretation is "thinking about emotional experiences" (1981, p. 178). Meltzer, along with Bion, believed that dreams and unconscious phantasy were synonymous (Spillius et al., 2011, p. 315).

When two personalities meet in the analytic space to talk together, emotional turbulence is generated and dreaming is stimulated. Symbols from dreams and unconscious phantasy tell many things of use for the psychoanalytic work. They not only substitute mental activity for action so that thinking can take place, but also enable sublimation, putting those perhaps impermissible primitive urges into thought and meaningful, culturally useful activities. Dreams also serve to access the creative imagination, the unconscious linking of images creating new ideas and new solutions, bypassing the ego. Creative people have shown us that "… what is essential and new in their creations came to them without premeditation and as an almost ready-made whole" (Freud, 1900a). It was noted by Freud that artists are more in touch with primary process phantasy than most people and consequently can draw on unconscious phantasy for their artistic creations. Dreams serve a communicative function between analyst and analysand, notifying both of the current state of the patient's unconscious and issues that need attention. I will present several dreams by patients in psychoanalysis to show their importance in revealing unconscious areas previously unsymbolised, containing important clues to their psychopathology.

Dream 1: the broken head

It is well known that first dreams are significant in revealing the central conflicts or dilemmas of the analysand. Soon after beginning analysis, an elegant middle-aged woman, distinguished in her field, unaccustomed to self-reflection, and whose internal world of emotion was unknown to her, told me that she dreamed that a small boy had been naughty and her eighteen-year-old son was hitting the boy's head repeatedly against a brick wall; his head was oozing with blood. My patient was standing by, urging him on, telling her son to do it harder, until the boy's head was broken open. When she awoke, she felt horror, guilt, and shame. This dramatic image told us, in the first place, of her anxiety about entering analysis and opening up her mind to our scrutiny: she feared what would happen, literally, to her head—the frightening concrete picture of psychoanalysis breaking her head open. We also got a first glimpse of her unconscious aggression, her cruel, punishing superego and a sadistic streak in her personality, about which she felt enormous guilt; all these were later to be elaborated and understood.

Dream 2: the queen and the soldier boy

A young woman began a session by saying she had had a dream but it was very difficult to remember. She got out of bed to write it down and then forgot it. Then she remembered the dream, which was about a princess who appeared out of a small door, as if from a cuckoo clock. "There was a man in the dream; I was there as an observer and the princess, who had a passionate nature, fell in love with the man. She felt herself melt in liquefying warmth. Then the princess with her umbrella took off and flew into the sky and I was on the ground, on a rock, cheering her on." Her associations were to a song about a queen and a soldier boy. In the lyrics the soldier knocks at the queen's door and she comes out. He tells her that he has been fighting in her war but now he wants to know why. He has seen many battles and people killed but most of the battles were lost and he doesn't want to fight any more. During the song she feels the warmth of the sun and melts emotionally but nevertheless she has him killed. In the exquisite longing she felt towards him, "she wanted more than she could ever say". Painful associations to this dream took place over a long period during which, in the transference and in her life, strong defences protected her from a fear that her ego would melt to extinction if she were to surrender to love; better to kill off the love object and remain in a state of longing.

Dream 3: dreams of sexual conflict

A series of dreams appeared in the material of a young woman who had recently married, and who had been struggling with her inhibitions and conflicts about sexuality and the wish for a child. After a long period of not dreaming, she had four dreams:

> I'm feeling much better today. I know I was angry and complained about H [her husband] last week, going on and on. I've had four dreams the last four days in a row; I can remember only parts, not all of them.

> In the first dream I was with H and another couple in their lounge; we were playing music and dancing around. I pulled up my skirt and was surprised I had on a thong. H said, "Those aren't proper knickers." I looked and realised only a tiny bit of my vagina was covered. Then I woke up.

> I was with another woman with long dark hair, about my age, I link her with an aggressive, envious woman that I know; we were chatting and there was a hint of the erotic. She said a friend was coming and the sexual tension heightened. Then a strange person came in, a fat man dressed in drag as a woman, with a white wig. He was disgusting; I felt sorry for him. He was sad and deflated and started talking about work.

> The following night I dreamed about Robert Redford, the name I call my gorgeous friend at work; others were there, a woman; it was a working day in the office. Though I knew he had a girlfriend, I went into a room with him; it felt warm and nice. He wanted me to cuddle him. I felt fond of him. We came out of the room and I felt afraid others might see us and I would get in trouble. He said something about his ex-girlfriend, I said, "Ex?" and he said, "Yes, ex." Then I woke up.

> In the dream I had last night I was kissing a friend's boyfriend. They were about to get married and I was thinking he was a good kisser. I guess that means I want sex, doesn't it? I was sick this morning and H asked me if it was morning sickness. We had decided a while ago not to use birth control and to try for a baby. Yes, in my dream about my vagina and knickers, having an opening there feels very uncomfortable. That's it really, my unease about sex. As an adolescent I got it all confused. Like I was defenceless against an angry penis, left with a vulnerable vagina. My body feels aroused and wants sex but my brain won't let me. I'm afraid that will always be my default position, yet I yearn for a baby, I have fantasies about it all the time. But I always want a different man than the one I'm with.

My patient's series of four dreams, discussed also in Chapter Seven on sexuality, tracked her shifting position in relation to sexuality and the narrative of her difficult conflicts and inhibitions around sex. In the first, she felt more relaxed about sexuality in the context of a pleasant evening with friends, but associations showed malaise. This led in the second dream to homoerotic feelings in relation to a woman, safer, perhaps envied, but then she shifted more excitedly towards the masculine, and a man appeared who turned out to be a degraded figure in drag towards whom she felt disgust and contempt. Moving away from these images as if rejecting homosexuality, she turned towards the sexy, desirable, idealised Robert Redford man in the third dream, who she thought was unavailable; he appeared tantalisingly single and tempting. In the fourth dream, she moved more clearly into the triangular situation, possibly enabling her to feel safer with a man and a woman, two figures representing parents. Feeling sexual desire, she kissed the fiancé of her friend, who was spoken for, off limits. I felt this demonstrated unresolved oedipal desires, the wish to take the man away from the woman, and helped me to understand her conflicts.

These dreams opened rich material that could be taken up as the analysis continued: her inhibitions and fears of sex, which she felt to be sadistic penetration; her contempt for men; her homoerotic urges, which were rejected; and her central oedipal dilemma, wanting to be in a sexual couple but afraid, always wanting a different man representing the unavailable father, but ultimately scared to take the mother's place and inhabit the role of oedipal couple by becoming a mother herself with a child of her own. In the transference, too, letting me in at times felt like an invasion, a harmful penetration, as we worked with her anxieties.

Conclusion

Dreaming relieves tension and internal discomfort. This is especially true when there has been a period of time in which dreams have not been remembered, as if remembering dreams and analysing them are important for psychic health. As Segal (1957) pointed out, contact with the unconscious through remembering dreams facilitates internal symbolic communication between consciousness and unconscious phantasy. When free symbol formation is facilitated and we can understand our symbolic language and think about our dreams, there is the possibility of greater mental integration, more movement in the mind, the repair of splits and objects. It is through symbols that we recapture, recreate, restore, and repair our objects (Segal, 1957, pp. 57–58), as well as find our enriched identity.

However, it must be underlined that it is not enough to simply dream if one is to use the insights available in dreams. Psychoanalysis is in agreement with the ideas of the philosopher Hegel in regard to the imagination. Hegel believed that "thinking in pictures" is a secondary form of thought to verbal thinking, so that images and pictures, and thus dreams, need to be put into words if they are to be used for thinking. Sensations, emotions, intuitions, and images, important as they are to mental life, are at their most useful when put to the service of consciousness and thought, and this is accomplished by translating them into meaning and into words.

In this chapter I have attempted to show that the production of symbolic imagery in the creative artist is essentially the same creative process as the production of dreams. As psychoanalysts, we study our patients in the search for unconscious phantasies that we believe are the basic building materials of the mind, phantasies that encapsulate symptoms and psychopathology, unavailable by direct contact but found through derivatives in dreams and symbolic representations. The psychoanalytic setting is designed to be a situation in which there is minimum interference from the controlling ego, in order to maximise the voice of the unconscious. While not always an aesthetic experience, dreams and their interpretation alter imagos and inner configurations, revealing, shifting, repairing, and integrating the internal world. Following our dreams, we too may evolve symbols, like Odilon Redon and his bouquet of flowers, representing confidence and joy in life.

The next chapter will continue the discussion of the potential for dream interpretation to restructure psychic reality, illustrated by a series of dreams in which the primal scene, repressed and viewed as destructive, appeared in the patient's dream material.

CHAPTER TEN

Dreams as access to the primal scene

In *The Interpretation of Dreams* (1900a), Freud extensively examined dream life and formulated his theories about the dream as infantile wish fulfilment, whereby unconscious repressed early memories or forbidden thoughts that evade censorship during sleep can appear in dreams, disguised by the dream work. In this chapter I will present a patient whose early experience formed unconscious phantasies of the primal scene that were symbolised in a series of dreams.

The patient, a bisexual woman with an obsessional personality, slept in the parental bedroom until the age of twelve. Dreams from her six-year analysis revealed the unconscious effects of her exposure to the primal scene and the evolution of the dream material is shown, moving from a phase of initial disguise into one of overt sexual content, then into dreams that indicated a modification of the early traumata that made possible working-through in the transference. I maintain that this process resulted in structural changes in her internal world; there was a shift in unconscious defences and inhibitions involving the patient's sexuality and sadism, modifying her obsessional anxiety and freeing her curiosity, to enable overall development to proceed.

Before presenting the patient's vivid dreams, I will briefly review the dream literature relevant to this patient. A more complete survey of dream theory was given in the previous chapter.

Brief review of the dream literature

For a period in psychoanalytic practice, dream interpretation had fallen into relative disuse as a primary clinical instrument. It was believed that the dream was suspect: it could be used defensively or as a gift to the analyst in order to distract him from difficult areas (Altman, 1975), or the dream could be used as a narcissistic production, calling attention away from object relations. In a re-evaluation of dream interpretation, Blum (1976) stated at an international symposium that the dream remained the keystone of mainstream clinical practice in the uncovering of infantile experience and in aiding reconstruction of past experience, noting how changes in its usage since Freud have been towards more transference interpretations of dream material. I fully agree with the view that dream interpretation is important in psychoanalysis, but would go much further than Blum, by proposing that work with dreams is responsible for promoting psychic change.

Studying the form and function of the dream as an indication of the structure of the personality was advocated by Segal (1986). She believed work with dreams was particularly important in the psychic process of "working through", taking the "good dreams" that appeared in the course of analysis as a sign of this process. Rycroft spoke of the dream as a "private, reflexive self-to-self communing" (1979, p. 46), which can be used to communicate with the analyst, tapping the dreamer's imagination to illustrate neurotic conflicts. Significantly, Meltzer (1983) believed that dreaming displays "narrative continuity" spread over the months and years of the analytic process. Padel (1987) emphasised that dreaming alters unconscious phantasy. The essential point was made by Klein (1935, 1940, 1946), Fairbairn (1943), and Guntrip (1961), that phantasy structures psychic reality, and that phantasy and structure are identical as psychic entities. Thus, it can be argued that consistent changes in dream symbolism over time are equivalent to the modification of unconscious phantasy and thus are indicative of inner psychic change, the view I represent.

Mrs R

The patient whose dreams I wish to consider, Mrs R, was forty-four years old when she decided to seek treatment for help with an acutely distressing situation. She had been married for twenty-two years in a partnership that was stable and companionable, seemingly happy enough although childless (a model marriage in the eyes of the couple's friends). Despite this, she had allowed herself to be pursued and seduced by a young lesbian actress, who, though a warm and charming person, was, unfortunately, a trophy collector of straight women whom she loved and then abandoned. Mrs R was heartbroken. Never having had an inkling before this intense affair that she might have been homosexual and, moreover, that it could be possible to be so emotionally tortured when the affair was breaking up and so totally bereft afterwards, she turned to analysis to help understand what had happened to her and why she had caused so many around her to suffer too.

Mrs R was the only child of a fussy, volatile, controlling father who worked as a civil servant, and a mother whose health was fragile and who was emotionally very tense and fearful. Her mother had eating difficulties, was often anorexic, and had frequent fainting spells during the patient's adolescence. Because of her mother's fragility, Mrs R could never go out to play during her childhood without returning regularly to ascertain that her mother was all right.

After she was born, Mrs R's mother was not well and she was looked after at home by a nanny or her maternal grandmother; they would disappear when father returned home in the evening. This routine went on until the patient was nearly a year old, forming a picture of maternal disruption and loss. Compounding her difficulties was the fact that the family lived in a small, three-room flat and Mrs R slept together with the parents in the only bedroom until she was twelve years old.

There were strict routines and rules for everything in the home, particularly around bedtime. She does not ever remember seeing her parents undressed, nor in any sort of sexual or affectionate embrace, and she particularly remembered a bedtime fantasy that when she closed her eyes at night it meant she would disappear. Sex was never mentioned, the night-time set-up never discussed, and Mrs R remembered insisting when speaking to childhood friends that her parents never engaged in sexual intercourse. In her mind parental sex was scotomized.

In adolescence, her previous keen interest in schoolwork ceased, and she poured her energies into theatrical performance and modern dance, which she practised obsessively. She went out with boys only because it was the thing one was supposed to do, but stopped seeing them as soon as they wanted her to become romantically or sexually involved. Denying knowledge of sexuality, she maintained a virginal image in her dress and demeanour, and in one of her early sessions she became aware that she had always idealised an image of herself as a pure, innocent four-year-old, untouched by the corruption of sex.

Her first sexual experience was with her husband-to-be, whom she met at college. She told me that she was determined to take the plunge into sex for the sake of getting married and that she found it pleasant enough, even exciting. Their sex life had continued but then had petered out a few years before she started analysis. Her husband was a kind, upright person, successful in a creative field and respected by his peers. Mrs R's work as a professional dancer and actress was enjoyable though not very successful, and she had never wanted children; she was haunted by fear and guilt that she had damaged her mother's health by being born and she didn't want to inflict this on herself or any children of her own.

When Mrs R began analysis, it became apparent that her personality was basically obsessional, characterised by defences of orderliness, tidiness, and control that manifested in her style in the session as well as life habits. She would come into the consulting room and place herself very precisely on the couch. After an initial silence of a minute or so, she would begin to speak in a calm and careful manner. After completing her thought she would stop speaking, allowing a silence while awaiting her next thought, and then, gathering and organising herself, she would speak again. The content included current activities; many memories of her childhood, adolescence, and adult life; and detailed portraits of her friends and family, always presented tidily, in a controlled manner, and without emotion as the good, quiet, little girl she was brought up to be. Such was the daytime version of her life that omitted any night-time spectres. I interpreted her defences against affect and her fear of strong emotion in various ways, as well as pointing out her good, compliant self in the sessions as a repetition of her compliance with the regime in her parental home. I also commented on how she protected me from any of her difficulties or emotions in the same way she had protected her fragile mother in childhood, and that she came to sessions to make sure I was all right.

Transference interpretations produced a surprised response and then denial, with the exception of work around holiday separations. She used me transferentially as an audience witnessing her performance in the sessions, a time that was used, she said, to relate to and explore herself. None of my interventions or their variations altered her basic modus operandi in the sessions. It was only through her vivid dream life that she began to communicate to me her striking inner dilemma: a network of anxiety-laden dream phantasies that derived from the primal scene. The first such dream occurred about a year after beginning therapy. It was as follows:

> This dream is like a story with a beginning, a middle, and an end. In a quiet Victorian house by the sea there was a mother, a father, and two children. I looked out at the sea and saw two enormous animals slowly splashing in the water, lifting their feet: one was like a rhinoceros, turned away—I couldn't see its head—and the other was like a mammoth without a trunk. In the house, I was holding the mother in my arms like a Victorian doll, when there was a disturbance on the beach. People were alarmed and gathering around. Swimmers were being pulled out of the water, sick and dying from something poisonous in the water. The rotting corpses were heaped under the window of the house and they began to bloat and grow larger, a fetid mound. The mother said that it was time to go to bed and began reading a bedtime story. The story book began with the sentence, "And then there were no more flowers, flowers, flowers ..." with the word "flowers" repeated to the bottom of the page. On the next page was, "And then there were no more trees ...;" on the next, "And then there were no more animals ...." Then I knew everyone would die of this plague and it would be the end of the world.

The dream has been called by Greenson (1970) "the freest of the free associations", since it evades internal censorship and control. When Mrs R told me the dream, her associations to its constituent parts and the whole followed, triggered off by its telling, so that the entire session would be a lattice of associations with the dream as its focus. Associations to this dream were to her childhood, her anxious, straitlaced mother, to bedtime stories read to her, to details of the shared bedroom, the arrangements of its furniture, and to the appearance of her parents as mounds in their bed as seen from her position in the bedroom. There were also associations to her husband, who would often make up stories to tell her before they went to sleep. I interpreted that the two huge animals represented her parents in bed at night when she was little and that, far from closing her eyes and not looking at them, she had watched them intensely. I made further comments that the dream was about her fear that her parents' sexual activities in bed were dangerous and toxic, a catastrophic end of the world: the fetid mound represented their poisonous sexuality, the missing parts of the animals represented her mother's missing penis and her father's penis disappearing into her mother, and the people dying in the water were dead babies produced by her parents' intercourse. I also linked the dream with anxious thoughts about having sex with her husband.

In the very next session she reported a dream, apparently linked to my statement in the previous session about looking intensely at her parents in bed. The dream was remarkable for its similarity to the dream of the *Wolf Man* recorded by Freud (Gardiner, 1972), in which there were several white wolves sitting in a tree looking into the house with large, staring eyes. Freud believed this dream heralded the uncovering of the roots of the Wolf Man's childhood obsessional neurosis in which the witnessing of parental intercourse at age one and a half was the main aetiological factor. Mrs R's dream was as follows:

> I was walking down the quiet street of my childhood home when out of a house came a beautiful black ocelot. It was staring at me with enormous glowing eyes that emanated colour, changing from red to blue to green, both separately and together. I felt frightened until a man came along who was the porter who lived in the basement flat of my home. He said, "This is the way to tame wild animals," at which point he lay on the ground, pulled up his shirt and let the animal smell his sweat. I thought this was very clever. The scene then became one in which a woman held a baby ocelot draped in her arms.

Her associations to this dream were to an occasion in her childhood when her father returned home tipsy from an office party, bringing with him into the bedroom a tiny kitten as a gift for her. Her mother, who had many phobias, one being cats, was horrified and angry, insisting that the kitten be taken out of the flat and given to the porter. Mrs R was terribly upset by this, as she had longed for a kitten. Other occasions when her father had been drinking came to mind, times when he would become playful and affectionate towards her mother, causing her to become annoyed and rejecting. Based on her associations to her childhood bedroom, I said that the ocelot in the dream symbolised her child self watching fearfully, while pretending to be asleep, as her father attempted to make love to her mother. And I said that the porter represented me, who was revisiting her childhood with her to tame her fears and to help her with the anxiety that had been aroused in her. I further interpreted in the transference that, in dreaming her early experience together with me, she can now feel safe, held like the baby ocelot in my arms. Her associations to this dream linked with her constant anxiety as a child that she was in her parents' home on sufferance, that she would be thrown out like the kitten if she broke the rules, including the tacit one that she "disappear" at night.

In the light of Meltzer's (1983) notion of "narrative continuity" in dreams and Rycroft's (1979) suggestion that dreams are communications that can be studied in sequence, with earlier dreams remembered by both patient and analyst, providing the context within which later dreams are interpreted, I became aware of a developing dream dialogue. A few weeks after the ocelot dream, Mrs R reported a dream with sexual content that was frank and less disguised, as follows:

I went outside and saw a parade of floats going by. On the first was a queen who was holding a briar wand in order to fend off the king, who was something in Greek with a name like "orgiastic paedophile". I wasn't sure about the words but I knew that it meant orgies with children. There was a voice-over, which was announcing the parade. The queen got off the float and began to dance but not very well, and I thought that I could do it better than she could. The voice-over then said, "On the next float is the king and he has gone over the top," and I saw that the float had nude children on it. And then I woke up.

In this dream, she associated the voice-over with me and the queen's dance with her desire to be a dancer but never feeling that she could dance well enough. I interpreted the king and queen in terms of the bedroom scene, saying that she had felt drawn into her parents' sexual activities, afraid that her father would make sexual advances towards her as well, and at the same time wishing that he would, feeling that she would be able to do it better than her mother. Again I linked the dream with her apprehensions about sex with her husband, believing she was too young, only a child.

Although Freud warned in *The Interpretation of Dreams* that associations to dreams cannot by any means be altogether dispensed with, he said of individuals in analysis that "… with the help of a knowledge of dream-symbolism it is possible to understand the meaning of separate elements of the content of a dream or separate pieces of a dream or in some cases even whole dreams, without having to ask the dreamer for his associations" (Freud, 1900a, p. 683). I had become familiar with Mrs R's imagination and dream symbolism so that the meaning of her dreams was immediately apparent, as Freud suggested. Following the dream about the king and queen, there was a series of frightening dreams about violent men who would invade her road, break into her flat, threaten her with dangerous electrical material, point guns at her, and men who would lose control, vomit and make a mess, expressing her unconscious equation of masculine sexuality with violence and disgusting loss of self-control. These were frightening phantasies that I interpreted as originating in the parental bedroom. Mrs R accepted all the primal scene dream interpretations with a sense of wonder and agreement.

Desire for and fear of sex was illustrated in a dream five weeks later, in which a college tutor, a teacher of "creative expression", was having sex with a fellow student, causing Mrs R to feel jealous. However, when he began to try to seduce her, she kicked him in the stomach and hurt him. He kissed her and his head turned into a skull with a light inside and she knew that he was the devil. She awoke with severe menstrual pains, which was unusual for her. In the session, the associations led to femininity and her feelings about being a woman, her fear of sex and pregnancy, and associations to women who were victims of men.

Four nights later Mrs R dreamed of a wonderful necklace given to her in the dream by her grandmother, whom she associated with me. It was made of tiny carved and painted ivory animals on a braided gold chain, which she associated with the therapy sessions. She put it on with another necklace that her husband had given her, made of rough raffia, which she associated with male sexuality. The two became tangled together, causing her distress. The dream changed to a scene in which she was having her long hair chopped off and she was left with thin red hair like a friend of hers who was in analysis and had broken down. This dream I interpreted as her fear that analysis would bring breakdown because of her anxiety about speaking of her night-time fears as a child, her fear of her parents' sexuality, and of sex with her husband. The fear of breaking down recurred from time to time and indicated the intensity of her early anxiety, her identification with her mother at night, and the shifts that were taking place in her defences.

The evolution that took place in Mrs R's dreams as a result of analysis showed that they were far from being random productions but consisted of themes that were woven into the ongoing dialogue with the unconscious. There was the theme of theft, which appeared three months later in a dream about a punk couple who were robbing neighbours in her childhood neighbourhood. Mrs R confronted them, saying, "Don't try it; people are watching." In this dream, the theme of watching linked with the ocelot dream, her stolen looks at her parents at night, and her role in the bedroom, watching them, which she believed would protect her mother from her father's sexual advances. There is the implication that sexual intercourse equals robbery: the phantasy that her mother was robbed of vitality by her father, rendered ill and unable to give physically or emotionally to her daughter.

Blum (1976) pointed out that, as analysis advances, the underlying conflict in a series of dreams may appear with increasingly less disguise in the manifest content. Nearly two months later my patient had an overtly erotic dream about her parents:

> I was with my parents and my father was making my mother put on a black corset with needles that stuck inwards. My mother had her clothes on. Then I realised that my father was beginning to press up against me, starting with his pelvis. I had my eyes closed and felt like a column of darkness. I decided to go along with it, relaxed completely, and experienced a wave of sexual pleasure. Then I stopped and felt very guilty, as if I had done something terrible and nothing would ever be the same.

The sadomasochistic excitement present in this dream upset her, along with its day residue, which was to do with a play she had seen the night before about a man who had sexually and violently abused his wife. I said that she had become sexually aroused as a child by what she believed to be sexual sadism between her parents, together with erotic feelings about her father, and that she felt very guilty about this.

Not only was the dream content altering in the direction of more direct sexual material, but dreams around the beginning of the third year of analysis began to alter in another way, wherein I began to appear in them undisguised. This was due, I believe, to changes in unconscious phantasy resulting from the previous interpretive work, indicating that the trauma of the primal scene was becoming clarified and was beginning to be worked through and replaced by the oedipal transference. I began to play a role in the internal drama. In my first undisguised appearance in her dreams, four days after the erotic dream about her father, she came to visit me but encountered an unfriendly husband who set up a dangerous obstacle. I interpreted this dream in a straightforward way as anxiety about being close to me as she was afraid my husband did not like it and would prevent her.

Several weeks later Mrs R had what she called a "paranoid" dream about me. We were together in her childhood bedroom, both in pyjamas and going to bed. I asked her for a special drink which she didn't have and I became annoyed, threatening to leave if she didn't go out to obtain it. In the dream she felt very anxious about this. I interpreted the dream by pointing out that in her mind I had taken her parent's place in the bedroom. Moreover, she felt that unless she complied with what I wanted, nourished and looked after me, I would reject her and break off our relationship. In the transference, I had become her needy, demanding mother and the demand to be nourished also indicated her own wish to have the breast to herself.

A third dream in which I appeared undisguised occurred four months later. She came to a session where I met her, saying goodbye to my husband, and led her to an incredibly messy bedroom, asking her to lie down on my husband's side of the bed, which she didn't want to do. She sat at the end of the bed feeling inexpressible sadness and I rubbed her chest in a gentle, soothing, non-erotic way, which she wanted me to go on doing forever. I interpreted that the mess stood for messy night-time sexuality, and that she both wanted and feared a seduction by me but that basically she wanted me as a mother, not a lover, to soothe her anxieties.

Her dreams trended towards not only an overall reduction of anxiety but changes in unconscious versions of sexuality that indicated release from repression and that working-through was taking place. Towards the end of the third year of analysis she reported a dream in which the night-time scene of her childhood appeared undistorted. The dream, almost like a memory, was of waking up in her childhood bedroom and hearing her parents in bed arguing. This dream indicated, to me, that the primal parental figures had become less saturated with terrifying phantasy and more realistic as a result of interpretive work.

A pleasant dream of the seaside occurred at the beginning of the fourth year, which contrasted markedly with the first seaside dream reported earlier. She was watching two men and a woman playing in the shallow water. The men were swinging the woman up into the air and letting her go, enabling her to fly. She would soar above the water, occasionally splashing into it and pushing off again. Mrs R was watching this scene with breathless fascination, urging the woman on. I pointed out that flying is often used as a metaphor for the feelings evoked by sexual intercourse, and that her dream was telling us that what men and women do together sexually now seems much less frightening.

Around this time, she resumed sexual relations with her husband and their marriage came to life, involving shared projects, travel, and being with friends. From time to time she thought with sadness about her lost lesbian lover but considered the affair to be part of a search for the nurturing mother of which she had felt deprived.

Throughout the last year of analysis there was a continuation of the working-through of the sadomasochistic theme, illustrated, for example, by a dream in the fourth year: a flirtatious girl waitress was seduced by an older man, after which she stuck a knife into the man's eye. This scene was observed by a prim, Victorian, older sister figure. I spoke of how she, by putting herself into the role of sister/observer, distanced herself from unacceptable parts of herself, in this case the flirtatious, sadistic girl in her.

Mrs R contacted me several years after the end of the analysis to say that she was well, her marriage was going well, and she had obtained a BA degree, which she had enjoyed, and was applying for postgraduate work. Later I heard that she had completed a PhD.

Discussion

Melanie Klein (1932) put forward the view that a primitive internal world is present at birth and is composed of instincts, anxieties, and defences in relation to primal objects. As the child matures, the primitive phantasy system is modified by experience, by contact with the external objects and environment, and undergoes various phases of psychic reorganisation and development. Areas of Mrs R's early internal world, disturbed by passions and frustrations in regard to desire for the mother's breast, entangled with tumultuous destructive phantasies of parental coupling, had become split-off and repressed, rendering the primitive objects unavailable for development. The primal scene was imbued with violent and sadomasochistic phantasies of parental intercourse, and these were intensified by her projected instinctual aggression, her jealous desire to possess mother's breast, her fear for mother's safety, and her oedipal fear and guilt, together with guilt about the dead babies. At the primitive level, sexuality and babies were calamitous, and this dissuaded her from having children of her own. Her unconscious anxiety was not present or available in the session material due to strong pre-conscious obsessional controls, but gained consciousness by means of dreams, "the return of the repressed". Dream analysis allowed working-through and integration, both at a conscious and unconscious level, and in the transference, bringing about structural change.

There were three consequences of the patient's repression of primal scene phantasies that hampered her emotional development, which should be mentioned. The first was the effect on her creativity of not being able to make a mess, to go into a creative regression in which reorganisation takes place and something new emerges. Mess or confusion were associated with the primal scene and activated her obsessional, controlling defences. The second was linked with the first: the patient's defences against sexuality and aggression, originating in the parental bedroom, prevented her passions from flowing into her work as a performer, sublimating them, infusing her work with primal energy and enlivening her performance. Excessive control prevented her from reaching the higher levels of artistic achievement that she had wanted. The third was the inhibition of curiosity, the looking, finding out, and knowing, that was forbidden in the parent's bedroom. This adversely affected her intellectual development, preventing her from looking freely and curiously at the world and learning for herself. The analytic enquiry, by focusing on understanding her internal world, released inhibitions and freed her curiosity, enabling her to take on new intellectual interests and to discover excitement in learning and insight, a new view of the world through her own eyes, the open eyes of the ocelot.

The next chapter will explore the way in which dreams played an important role in the analysis of a paedophile, marking the turning point in the treatment.

CHAPTER ELEVEN

Arrested development: notes on a case of paedophilia

The path of emotional development sometimes goes awry and reaches the cul-de-sac of sexual perversion. For the paedophile presented in this chapter, sexual contact with young boys was his consuming interest. The study of sexual perversion has become a pressing issue, as we have been made aware of the extent of child sexual abuse in our society. I will begin by outlining theories from the psychoanalytic literature before presenting the case and the discussion.

The psychoanalytic literature

Many of the contributions to the literature on the aetiology of perversion point to the disturbance of the early relationship to the primal object in regard to excess innate aggression, including acute infant self/object confusion, bodily fusion states, terror of loss of the object or self, and the resultant desperate distancing mechanisms that are an attempt to differentiate and maintain a sense of self against the fear of ego disintegration and non-survival—a fear thought to be shared by all the perversions (Gallwey, 1978; Glasser, 1979, 1986; Khan, 1979; McDougall, 1972, 1986; Stoller, 1976). These authors also refer to the style of communication in perversions—disturbances in symbolic functioning, concrete thinking, omnipotent autistic domination of the object, and excessive use of projective identification—indicating severe disturbances in object relationships, together with interference with thinking and reality testing.

Most psychoanalytic writers treat the perversions as a unitary phenomenon, discussing the features shared by all the perversions. Meltzer (1973) wrote of four features that are characteristic: inhibited genital sexuality, inadequate identifications, strong defences against depressive anxiety, and a sadomasochistic narcissistic organisation. He noted an absence of dependence on the internal parental couple in which the mother functions as nurturer and container for persecutory anxiety and the father's penis functions as a protector of mother's body and her babies. Instead, anxiety is regulated by means of the deviant sexual act in which there is a triumphant abolition of depressive and even persecutory anxiety. Meltzer wrote of the presence in the internal world of a "stranger" who hates the primal scene and creativity.

Khan (1979) discussed the use of the sexual object in the perversions as an "as-if transitional object" directed against anxiety states in an act of reparation to the self, creating an infant idolised by the mother. He stressed the importance of power and will as a defence against psychic pain, rage, sadism, and hate. Stoller (1976) stressed the role of phantasy in creating the aberrant sexual choice and the responsibility that the sexual deviant holds for the wilful formation of his own deviancy.

Glasser (1988) was one of the few writers who focused on the specific psychodynamics of paedophilia. He observed that paedophiles experience the need for love and intimacy as annihilatory: they fear being taken over totally. It is felt to be too dangerous to make identifications with parental objects that would enable the development of an adult self-structure to take place, because of a fear of invasion and possession. The paedophile, fuelled by an inordinate degree of castration anxiety, defends against the catastrophe of fusion or possession by narcissistic withdrawal, self-preservative aggression, and the domination and control of objects such that they are given no independent existence. The paedophilic act bestows upon the child self the love that the paedophile was deprived of, without the necessity for a real relationship.

The theories concerning the paedophile's preferred object choice (babies, young children, or older children), the type of contact (penetrative sex or masturbatory activity), and why paedophilia is preferred to incest, homosexuality, fetishism, phobias, or other conditions attributed to castration anxiety, can be inferred from psychoanalytic developmental models. Penetrative sex and the disorders stated above are seen as more advanced in terms of psychosexual development, in which some degree of negotiation and resolution of oedipal anxieties has taken place. One central issue is the degree of innate aggression that contributes, through projective identification, to the extreme degree of castration anxiety, driving the personality to defensive splitting and a massive retreat from oedipal and genital object relating.

Mr L

At age thirty-five, Mr L, a slim, attractive man working in a profession, had approached his GP to ask for treatment for his compelling need to go to parks and pick up pre-teenage boys, whom he would then undress and engage in masturbatory activities. He felt that he must stop this, being troubled by his fear of arrest by the police. The consulting psychiatrist first sent him for behavioural treatment, which included aversion therapy, wherein penile shock was applied while viewing images of prepubescent boys, then withdrawn when shown images of women. The patient had experienced this treatment as humiliating, painful, and completely useless. Wishing to pursue help for his problem, he was offered private psychoanalytic psychotherapy with me, which he took up rather reluctantly, insisting that he could pay only a low fee.

On first starting treatment, Mr L refused my attempts to help him tell his story and spent his time either in turgid silence or, alternatively, in arguments and attempts to convince me that sex with children should be allowed. He believed that society was mistaken in its values and laws—the Ancient Greeks had it right. The paedophile's principal desire, he claimed, was to make boys happy, to give them love and affection, and he fantasised about utopian countries in which sex with children was permitted. His arguments were apparently based on the assumption that all children were as bereft of affection in boyhood as he had been.

As I repeatedly commented on his reticence in speaking of himself and his life, Mr L began to describe his childhood in a stilted and broken way, small bits at a time, occasionally tearfully, describing the terrible loneliness and isolation that he had experienced as the third and last child of busy professional parents who seemed to have nothing to give him emotionally.

In his account, his parents had had no patience with his awkwardness and helplessness, or with his inability to play with other children or to join in happily on almost any sort of occasion. The images were desolate and depicted a passive, helpless, extremely unhappy little boy, able to take very little of what was available or given. He spoke of his brother's cruel treatment of him and his, and other children's, refusal to play with him; he described the humiliation of consistently being chosen last when teams were formed for games. His best friend and closest companion was the family dog, and he remembered being broken-hearted when it died. His mother's authoritarian treatment of him would only be shaken when, occasionally, he would make a huge fuss and then get his own way. He felt this was entirely unsatisfactory because, whatever had been the issue, he felt his mother had not given in to him willingly because she loved him, but only because of his loud protests. Whenever his parents would try to joke with him and tease him out of his ill humour, he would become even more sulky and infuriated. Reparation and forgiveness were not part of his repertoire; his rejection of the adult world was complete. He reported curious mental states of passivity as a child, when he would be lying still, completely unable to move a muscle in spite of desperately trying, until someone— the au pair or his brother—would come along and touch or rouse him.

There were some areas of good object relationship that he would get in touch with from time to time. His sister, ten years older and mostly away at boarding school, was kind to him. His GP father would take him on house calls, and he remembered waiting for him in the car, although when he became impatient he would, in despair, tear at the upholstery in the back seat with a penknife. Music was his means of contact with his father—a father otherwise subdued and withdrawn, dominated at home by his mother. His link to his father was inarticulate and formal, but he would lie under the piano, or in a play fortress, listening while his father played classical music. He was given piano lessons but would stop playing if anyone came into the room or complimented him, refusing to give pleasure to others or to please them. After beginning therapy, he bought a piano and began to play again, and much of our language in the transference was of musical imagery and metaphor. Another memory he returned to again and again was of an idealised time during the summer holidays, when he had met a boy who had chosen him as a playmate, and together they had spent an idyllic hour playing games on the beach—a reflection of the analytic hour. At boarding school he fell in love with several of the boys his age and older, and he realised that it was not only the sex play that drew him.

He would follow them around, feeling emotionally dependent and needy in relation to them. He knew even then that he would not outgrow his love for boys.

His early relationship with his mother was depicted in a screen memory in which he approached her while she sat reading, and, unable to get her attention, he bit her on the ear. This so angered her that she grabbed him and bit him back. He remembered being extremely hurt and upset by this, and from then on he completely turned away from his mother emotionally. I understood this screen memory to refer to his primal infant object relationship with his mother—a violent, mutually attacking, bad relationship, which was later to appear in the transference, compounded with castration fears.

At about the eighteen-month point in the therapy there was a critical juncture. Mr L became disillusioned with the treatment and lost hope in it as a means of changing his sexual orientation. Up to this point, his sexual outlet was to masturbate on the weekends while smoking cannabis and having fantasies of boys. Incited by the news of a proposal in the Netherlands to lower the age of consent for homosexuals, he began to hint that he was going to return to the active practice of paedophilia. His threat to begin picking boys up again presented me with a conflict: if I maintained a neutral stance, he would resume his sexual activities with boys, yet if I took a stand against it, we would re-enact the scenario with his forbidding, possessive mother. As much for my own ethical needs as anything else, I said that if he were to start again, I would not be able to continue to see him, as paedophilia was not only against the law but against what I felt to be good for boys. I told him that I could not continue to help him if it would mean helping him to break the law and go against my beliefs. He produced arguments against this, struggled with his anger and despair, but gradually seemed to accept it. Of course, I could never be completely sure that he was not picking up boys, but his reproachful hatred towards me subsequently suggested that perhaps he was not.

I worked interpretively on the link between me and his mother: that he felt I deprived him of all pleasure of any kind and that I wanted to dominate him. My stand against his return to paedophilic acts was accompanied by my repeated emphasis on his need for help—a need relating to his whole life, not simply to his sexual orientation.

After this period, the climate in the sessions, which had always been difficult, became extremely uncomfortable. He often retreated into aloof silence, during which I would experience feelings of isolation, constriction, and despair. I interpreted that this silent rejection of me was loneliness put into me to show me how alone and snubbed he had felt as a child, deprived of friendly contact. I continued to try to interpret, in the transference, his wishes for me to care for him and his child self, while at the same time interpreting his fear of me and his angry, destructive feelings towards me and the therapy.

As the therapy continued, his discontent extended to the fees, which I increased by a small amount annually. Each time I put them up he was hurt, upset, and withdrawn, feeling that it meant that I did not care about him and was only using him for my own needs. Yet, little by little, the story of his emotionally arid life continued to unfold, and after about five years he began to tell me his dreams. There were many of terrifying female figures: monster women with tentacles or snakes for breasts, evil, wild-haired women with a missing arm or leg, waiting for him in a cave or at the end of a tunnel. I interpreted these as images of me, his horror of being with me, a woman, someone without a penis. He had memories that revealed sexual confusion and anxiety about his body. He would not take his shirt off at the beach because he was convinced that his body looked like a girl's, with skinny arms and heavy hips and legs. When I suggested that it was upsetting to him when he discovered that little girls don't have a penis, he responded with a memory of being excruciatingly embarrassed and upset at seeing a little girl, a visitor to the family home, naked in the bathtub with the adults gathered around. His mother urged him to join her in the bath, but he refused, feeling terrified that he would lose his penis and that his body would become just like hers.

Another memory in relation to his mother emerged in connection with an event that was crucial to the formation of his paedophilia and was to play a significant role in the treatment. At about age six he had been caught playing sexual games with two other boys. Instead of admonishing him at the time of the incident, his mother had waited until bath time. As she was drying him off, standing over him while he was naked and vulnerable, she severely reprimanded him, telling him that he must never play such games again. After he had his pyjamas on and was in bed, she came to his bedside and ran her hand up his pyjama leg as if to go for his penis, terrifying him. This incident made him feel that his mother was claiming him sexually for herself and wanted his penis; he marked this as the beginning of his real terror of women as sexual beings. This led to a dramatic focus in the transference around his fear that I would try to claim him or his penis for myself. Was this why mother/I was trying to stop him from playing sexually with boys?

Other writers treating paedophilic patients have made observations of deadness in the transference and inarticulate silences, and these persisted in my patient. To a comment I might make on his aloof withdrawal, he would respond archly, "Someone has tampered with my soul, and I must hide away to be safe and secure," strikingly illustrating Steiner's "psychic retreat", a defence based on grievance and revenge, smouldering, clung to, and even regarded by the patient as a strength and purpose (Steiner, 1993).

In Mr L's retreat, he was isolated within his internal world, and this was illustrated by a dream:

I was alone in a cold, dead, grey forest surrounded by small, blind, armoured creatures, like armadillos or turtles, creeping aimlessly and slowly at random around me. I came upon a little glass box that was emitting light and colour and exciting images. When I looked into it, I saw that it was the social world of people talking and being together. I felt excluded, but I didn't want to have anything to do with it.

I interpreted this dream as his putting me under his control, enclosing me in the glass box, while he shut himself off from me and remained alone in his dead inner world, wanting but refusing to link up. As we worked on this dream material, unbearable feelings of non-existence or overwhelming sleepiness were induced in me and made me feel like one of his blind, stupid, meaningless creatures from the dead forest. In this way he dehumanised us both, and eventually I began to understand this as his trying to expel bad feelings into me instead of experiencing and thinking about his problems and how to talk to me. As I spoke to him of these things, he remained wooden and armoured, while I continued to experience the painful deadness that was both an attack on my thinking function and a communication of his blind, cold, dead internal world in which he would allow nothing to live. I pointed out that this was a way of showing me how shut out, helpless, and angry he had felt as a child. I also suggested that it gave him relief to push these painful feelings into me, ridding himself of them, leaving me to deal with them and seeing whether I could bear them.

He then brought three short dreams that marked a significant change in the therapeutic relationship. I understood the change as having been brought about by the consistent work on his anxiety about linking with me, with the analysis of his symbolic material representing a link between us, and the attempt on my part to relate to his child self:

> Two boys were in bed; I was one. I began stroking the other one and he turned into a girl or, perhaps, I thought, a castrated boy. I went to ask permission from someone to be in bed with her.

> A cat was tied to a post, starving. A scientist was looking on, waiting to see what the cat would do, either eat a poisoned chocolate mouse that was offered to it or starve.

> A frozen, tattered, disfigured old woman, starving, with skin like a chicken leg, was told by a scientist that she had just spent all her money, millions, on jewellery.

The first dream indicated that Mr L was beginning to accept me as a woman and could tolerate being with me in the session, but he needed permission. However, in the second dream he was clearly playing a game of cat and mouse with me, cruelly attacking me with his passivity, revengefully starving himself of emotional nourishment before my eyes and deriving pleasure from it. When I said this to him, he gave a smile. I was clearly the mouse, poisoned by his projected anger, and he was afraid to take anything that I offered, making me, in the third dream, into a tattered, disfigured, frozen, starving old woman with nothing to give him. I could not disguise my anger at this point, saying that he was self-destructively starving himself in front of me, expecting me to stand by and watch, like the scientist in the dream, and this affected him. He admitted that he wanted to row with me and told me how, as a child, he would provoke his mother into anger and then get upset by it. At the end of that session he asked for an increase in the number of sessions per week, from two to three.

The following week he brought another dream:

> I was inside a round stone building that had all the windows and doors bricked up. I was alone, with nothing to do but eat a plate of unappetising porridge that had grit in it. I knew I could try to escape, but I was afraid that jailers would chase and capture me.

I interpreted that by increasing the sessions he felt closer to me but this was scary. I said that he had retreated into a stone building without openings so I couldn't touch him, but this felt like a jail. Moving closer to me meant that I would take him over and imprison him; he felt terrified that I would penetrate into his lonely world and into his body, the price of the security of being safely held in the therapy/prison. Inside the walls he could imagine himself to be self-sufficient and in omnipotent control of me and the therapy, although this meant emotional malnutrition.

During the next two years Mr L felt somewhat more present in the therapy, but I consistently needed to focus on his anxiety about being close to me and how this aroused aggressive and violent feelings towards me. He had frightening and destructive dreams that he took pleasure in—for example, in one dream two huge alien spaceships were shooting at each other and he felt pleased about the destructiveness. Then he would deaden himself or make himself soporific in a passive defence against anger and violent feelings, reporting dreams in which we were fused together as a giant slug in a defensive merging. I was both a persecuting absence between sessions and a persecuting presence in sessions.

I understood the material during this period to relate to a battling internal parental couple, as well as attacks on our coupling in the therapeutic relationship. However, a number of his dreams during this period were also reparative, as when, for example, he dreamed about reconstructing a house and building new structures on dilapidated buildings. He continued to use me as a vessel into which he projected his bad feelings of helplessness, hopelessness, and fury, wishing to induce me to become enraged and attack him, thus enacting with him his sadomasochistic, internal object relationships. He agreed that if I did attack him, he would then be able to feel something in relation to me. It became clear that having affectionate feelings towards me, or even speaking openly with me, was terrifyingly dangerous and would lead to—and was unconsciously equivalent to—a violent, castrating sexual relationship. Here was his fundamental confusion between sex, affection, and aggression. When I said that he didn't know what an affectionate relationship with me would feel like, he said, in his aloof way, "Something like white noise—soothing in a way."

As time went on, I began to have more of a containing existence for him. He told me about his present life, his problems at work, his relationships with his boss and colleagues, and his struggle to get a promotion.

Gradually, he began to speak of wanting more from me, saying that he was afraid I did not care about him. He liked me to remember what happened in previous sessions; it made him feel cared-about to know that I kept him in mind. He admitted to feeling abandoned between sessions, not liking the fact that we stopped on time, wanting to go on, wanting to be my favourite. He dreamed of a child in prison who was being rescued, clearly his own child self being rescued, becoming freer and making contact. He complained that each session was too difficult to begin and that he felt the ending to be a painful rejection, bearable only if he deadened himself and did not allow spontaneous feeling. Yet he was slowly becoming better at tolerating the pain of need, loss, and separation, and his expression of these feelings and my empathic responses marked a more open feeling in the analytic space, often to close up again. When I would speak about his difficulty in taking something good away, to hold on to between sessions, he said that if he were to do that it would make everything ordinary between us, indicating, I thought, his feeling of magical control, of bringing me to life in the sessions and giving me no separate existence.

Evidence of his splitting appeared in a dream during the eighth and last year of treatment, which Mr L remembered in response to my saying how hard it was for him to see me as someone on his side. He dreamed of two houses side by side. In one was a boy with large genitals, masturbating; in the other was a dangerous, powerful woman. I said that the houses were him and me, side by side, to which he replied that both houses were parts of him that he kept separate, representing sexuality and anger. If they were joined together, there would be "murderous sexuality". "Yes", I responded, "that is how you see your parents' sexual intercourse, as terrible murderous sexuality."

In subsequent sessions he went on to connect shame, guilt, and disgust with adult sexuality: he stated, "Sexual feelings between adults is perverse," and he had a dream of his parents having violent, disgusting sexual intercourse, smearing shit. After a visit from his parents, during which he experienced his mother as still dominating and manipulative towards him, he said to me openly for the first time that he hated her and later reported a wish that he could kill them both.

It was unfortunate that therapy had to end prematurely when his company sent him abroad to work. The ending phase was painful and he was tearful when he acknowledged his dependency on me and the significance of our relationship. He asked me to write to him, which I did, sending him at his request the name of a psychotherapist in the southern European city to which he had moved.

Discussion

I would like to examine Mr L's psychoanalytic therapy as it revealed and recapitulated features of his development and object relationships. It has been noted by many writers that all of the perversions have in common severe sexual anxiety and unconscious sexual guilt (Welldon, 1996), although consciously Mr L's paedophilia was ego-syntonic. His sexual anxiety encompassed all psychosexual relations, from the primary infant–mother relationship to the anal battle for control, the oedipal arena, and the primal scene. I believe his anxiety stemmed from unconscious guilt about his hatred, aggression, and overthrow of parental authority at every level. Mr L told me how, in a desperate bid to be normal during adolescence, he had made several traumatic attempts to date girls. They all ended in complete failure, helplessness, and humiliation, a cul-de-sac that resulted in the blocking-off of heterosexual development and the directing of his libido towards prepubescent boys—the age before the bodily changes due to the influx of adolescent sexuality and aggressivity occur. His disgust and hatred of the primal scene, containing his own projected genital sexuality and aggression, resulted in a sexualisation of all relationships, which was confirmed when he told me that he had sex in fantasy with everybody he met. His hatred of the devouring, castrating mother made contact with me nearly impossible in the early period of treatment. As oedipal material began to show up in the treatment during the last year, it was unfortunate that Mr L was sent abroad before sufficient working-through could take place.

The second feature of Mr L's personality that I want to discuss is his problem of self-identity, also noted as a feature in these patients by others who have worked with perversions. Due to splitting and projection of his needy, aggressive, dependent, and vulnerable selves, there was extreme identity confusion. Freud (1914c) wrote of the failure of paedophiles and homosexuals to project primary narcissism onto the father and then to identify with him, so providing the basis for a sense of self as an adult male. In Mr L's development, childhood narcissism was retained and transformed into the ideal child self. His father's protective aspects, stripped of humanness, were internalised as music and used narcissistically to cancel out the father's sexual, oedipal function.

Without a containing maternal figure as well, there were not the female identifications that can be found in homosexual development, in which sexual conflict is resolved by incorporating a creative feminine receptivity that allows an internal space and the foundation for fertile interrelationships. I believe that although Mr L's love for boys could be seen as a substitute for oedipal love for his father, he did not become homosexual for fear of encountering an adult penis that would make him feel even smaller and more humiliated. As the idealised child self, Mr L established for himself an identity based on a sense of his own moral superiority in relation to what he felt was the vicious, depriving adult world.

He thus omnipotently regulated his own self-esteem, enabling himself by this means to have some sense of stability and integrity. In the paedophilic act, he repaired his wounded self-image, idealising and nurturing his deprived child self by ritually undressing and masturbating boys. In this act of reversal, the humiliation and forbidden sexuality at the hands of his mother was erased, and he could triumphantly establish himself as projected into an adored little boy, on whom attention and affection were lavished. In doing this—which he consciously rationalised as a loving act—he could act out a hidden, unconscious, vengeful attack on his mother and her babies. The sexual parents and the adult world, hated persecutory objects, were split off and projected, together with his own hateful and uncaring child parts, while his idealised child self served to contain the psychotic anxiety of his fragmented child self, helping him to survive the threat of disintegration.

I experienced Mr L's early transference to me as perverse, in that every attempt to engage with and contact him was met with lofty silence and aridity. I felt in the countertransference annoyance, deadness, and an excruciating sense of the constriction and emptiness of his internal world. Labelled "transference perversion" by Etchegoyen (1978), these patients form, a therapeutic relationship characterised by passivity, the provocation of irritation and impatience in the analyst, and the projection of painful feelings both defensively and as attacks (Joseph, 1971). Defiance and rebellion in the transference has been noted (Etchegoyen, 1978), defeating the attempt to form a therapeutic alliance. Stubborn rebellion was powerful in my patient; the wrongness of the paedophilic act, he admitted, provided much of the excitement, repeating a childhood situation of always being in the wrong in his family. I was the target for his sadomasochistic perverse transference against dangerous object-relating and depressive anxiety. The perverse transference could also be construed as Mr L's sadistic wish to enact with me his destructive phantasy relationships in which he sought revenge on his depriving, hated objects. The absence of good internal objects meant that each session was an encounter with a hated, dreaded person, who must be put off, obscured, obfuscated. Glasser (1988) mentioned the quality of "dullness" in the paedophile that interferes with the therapist's mentation. Gallwey (1978), too, spoke of the heaviness or dullness in the countertransference by which the patient conveys trapped and claustrophobic anxiety, with negativism and mental paralysis, representing a petrified area of the patient's mind that protects him from his need for others. The sexual act brings the paedophile back to life, counteracting narcissistic and psychotic anxieties, and omnipotently establishing himself as the perfect child.

The inner deadness in Mr L was, I think, due in a large part to immense hatred and aggression towards his needy child self, in an attempt to obliterate it. My interpretative focus was on his projection of poisonous and dead mental states, on aggression and rage towards me and towards his parents, and his neediness, expressed primarily passively in destructive negation, a refusal to take whatever was offered in childhood and in the therapy. His aggression was linked to his envy of my ability to think and to care—the food that therapy could offer him. As he became aware in the therapeutic relationship of how aggressive he was towards me, and found that I could accept and tolerate it, he felt understood and began to tolerate his own need of me and my containing function.

Mr L's propensity for denying reality was maintained by splitting and projection (of, for example, his hated adult self, his disgust of his own sexuality, or himself as a needy child). When he erased the differences between himself and children, he created a situation that constituted a psychotic overthrow of reality. Then, when he came back into contact with the denied reality, he was further maddened by its intransigence as he faced the inevitable truth that he was not actually a child and paedophilia was illegal.

As long as Mr L could identify with the idealised child, the loss and damage of childhood was denied, and mourning and reparation were blocked. As the therapeutic work proceeded, some experiences in the transference of separation, loss, and need were tolerated by him. In the therapeutic relationship, as he began to re-introject a more intact child self, aided by empathic and symbolic linking with me, Mr L's internal dilemma became more available, appearing in dreams. I believe that his poison mouse dream and my emotional response was a turning point, when he began to feel that I actually did care for him. When he had the stone house dream, there was more of a feeling of containment and security in the therapy, but still an illusion of omnipotent control over me as a defence. In the next period of the work, his dreams of violence seemed to signal a sense of a separate self in attack on a separate, uncontrollable object, and his primal scene dreams revealed the source of his hatred. Following this, reparative dreams and more intimate disclosures in regard to his day-to-day life appeared in the sessions. Because of my tolerant interpretations of his aggressive projections and his attempts to kill me off, I believe I began to be experienced by him as someone with a real separate personal existence and therefore as able to contain him. During the last eighteen months, he could express dependency and a sense of loss and separation between sessions.

Therapeutic change

Change in therapy is signalled by the renunciation of narcissism in favour of dependence on good objects, as pointed out by Meltzer (1967) and others. Whole-object relating becomes possible at the threshold of the depressive position, introjective processes predominate in psychic reality, and the excessive use of projective identification is given up. A working-through of the Oedipus complex can then take place. For Segal (2007), therapeutic change takes place as the fragmented object is transformed by projection and re-introjection in the therapeutic exchange, enabling the patient to internalise a more whole and intact object, with ambivalence as a factor.

How much structural change actually occurred in his therapy was uncertain, but Mr L was able to make more emotional contact with me and to express some need and dependency. However, it was impossible to tell how much introjection of the therapy, of me and my concern for him, was allowed and how much of his intense anxiety about relating was worked through. He certainly continued his use of projective mechanisms until the end.

Although he relinquished some of his omnipotent defences and was able to have some depressive-position experiences, Mr L continued to feel disappointed that his desire for sex with boys was still active and that I prevented him from having this pleasure. He would talk in his stilted way about friendships that he would attempt to have, but it was difficult to tell whether his relationships actually improved. Once I came across him in my neighbourhood, speaking vivaciously to a woman. I was amazed by this evidence of his splitting, seeing in him a lively and fluently talkative person who was completely different from the deadened self he displayed in the sessions. In the therapy some modification, I believe, was made of his fearsome primal objects, his splits and projections, and his fear of aliveness, and I thought I could see some sign of the formation within him of an inner space, not deadly, but one that held the possibility of life and growth.

REFERENCES

Abraham, K. (1911). Notes on the psycho-analytical investigation and treatment of manic-depressive insanity and allied conditions. In: *Selected Papers on Psychoanalysis* (pp. 137–156). London: Karnac, 1988.

Abraham, K. (1919). A particular form of neurotic resistance against the psychoanalytic method. In: *Selected Papers on Psychoanalysis* (pp. 303–311). London: Karnac, 1988.

Abraham, K. (1920). The narcissistic evaluation of excretory processes in dreams and neurosis. In: *Selected Papers on Psychoanalysis* (pp. 218–322). London: Karnac, 1988.

Abraham, K. (1921). Contributions to the theory of the anal character. In: *Selected Papers on Psychoanalysis* (pp. 370–392). London: Karnac, 1988.

Abraham, K. (1924). A short study of the development of the libido, viewed in the light of mental disorders. In: *Selected Papers on Psychoanalysis* (pp. 418–501). London: Karnac, 1988.

Abram, J. (2005). L'objet qui survit (trans. D. Alcorn). *Journal de la Psychanalyse de l'Enfant*, 36: 139–174.

Altman, L. (1975). *The Dream in Psychoanalysis*. New York: International Universities Press.

Asch, S. S. (1976). Varieties of negative therapeutic reaction and problems of technique. *Journal of the American Psychoanalytic Association*, 24: 383–407.

Begoin, J. (1998). Review of the book "Reason and Passion: A Celebration of the Work of Hanna Segal". *International Journal of Psychoanalysis, 79*: 819–821.

Bell, D. (2002). I am the spirit that negates all: Negation, the active principle of Thanatos [unpublished paper].

Bion, W. R. (1957). Differentiation of the psychotic from the non-psychotic personalities. In: *Second Thoughts* (Chapter Five, pp. 43–64). London: Karnac, 1967.

Bion, W. R. (1959). Attacks on linking. I n: *Second Thoughts* (Chapter Eight, pp. 93–109). London: Karnac, 1967.

Bion, W. R. (1962). *Learning from Experience*. London: Karnac, 1984.

Bion, W. R. (1963). *Elements of Psycho-Analysis*. London: Karnac, 1984.

Bion, W. R. (1965). *Transformations: Change from Learning to Growth*. London: Tavistock.

Bion, W. R. (1967). *Second Thoughts: Selected Papers on Psychoanalysis*. London: Maresfield [reprinted London: Karnac, 1984].

Bion, W. R. (1970). *Attention and Interpretation: A Scientific Approach to Insight in Psychoanalysis and Groups*. London: Karnac.

Bion, W. R. (1992). *Cogitations*. London: Karnac.

Birksted-Breen, D. (2003). *Sexuality in the Consulting Room*. Paper presented at the 25th International Anna Freud Centre Colloquium, London: Has sex left psychoanalysis?

BirkstedBreen, D., Flanders, S., & Gibeault, A. (Eds.) (2010). Introduction to *Reading French Psychoanalysis* (pp. 1–25). London and New York: Routledge.

Blum, H. (1976). The changing use of dreams in psychoanalytic practice: Dreams and free association. *International Journal of Psychoanalysis, 57*: 315–324.

Brenman, E. (2006). *Recovery of the Lost Good Object*. London and New York: Routledge.

Britton, R. (1998). *Belief and Imagination*. London and New York: Routledge.

Britton, R. (1999). Getting in on the act: The hysterical solution. *International Journal of Psychoanalysis, 80*: 1–14.

Britton, R. (2003). Narcissistic problems in sharing space. In: *Sex, Death and the Superego* (pp. 165–178). London: Karnac.

Britton, R. (2008). What part does narcissism play in narcissistic disorders? In: J. Steiner (Ed.), *Rosenfeld in Retrospect: Essays on his Clinical Influence* (Chapter Three, pp. 22–34). London and New York: Routledge.

Britton, R. (2013). *The Love that Dare Not Speak Its Name*. Paper presented to UCL Conference on Enactment, London, December 2013.

Britton, R. (2015). *Between Mind and Brain: Models of the Mind and Models in the Mind*. London: Karnac.

Chasseguet-Smirgel, J. (1974). Perversion, idealization and sublimation. *International Journal of Psychoanalysis, 55*: 349–358.

Diena, S., & Serrati, B. (2008). *Identity and change: the function of creativity in the search for identity.* Paper presented at the European Psychoanalytic Federation Conference, The Shadow of Heritage, Vienna.

Druick, D. (1994). *Odilon Redon 1840–1916.* London: Thames & Hudson.

Etchegoyen, R. (1978). Some thoughts on transference perversion. *International Journal of Psychoanalysis, 59*: 45–53.

Fairbairn, W. R. D. (1943). The repression and the return of bad objects. In: *Psychoanalytic Studies of the Personality* (pp. 59–81). London: Tavistock, 1952.

Fairbairn, W. R. D. (1952). *Psychoanalytic Studies of the Personality.* London: Tavistock.

Fenichel, O. (1945). *Psychoanalytic Theory of Neurosis.* New York: Norton.

Ferenczi, S. (1931). Trauma and anxiety. In: M. Balint (Ed.), *Final Contributions to the Problems and Methods of Psycho-Analysis* (trans. Mosbacher) (pp. 249–50). London: Hogarth.

Fonagy, P. (1991). Thinking about thinking: Some clinical and theoretical considerations in the treatment of a borderline patient. *International Journal of Psychoanalysis, 7*: 639–656.

Fonagy, P. (2008). A genuinely developmental theory of sexual enjoyment and its implications for psychoanalytic technique. *Journal of the American Psychoanalytic Association, 56*: 11–36.

Fonagy, P., & Target, M. (1994). Understanding and the compulsion to repeat: A clinical exploration. *Bulletin of the Anna Freud Centre, 17*: 33–55.

Fonagy, P., Steele, M., Steele, H., Moran, G., & Higgitt, A. (1991). The capacity for understanding mental states: The reflective self in parent and child and its significance for security of attachment. *Infant Mental Health Journal, 12*: 201–218.

Freud, S. (1900a). *The Interpretation of Dreams. S. E., 5*: 613–686. London: Hogarth.

Freud, S. (1905d). *Three Essays on the Theory of Sexuality. S. E., 7*: 123–246. London: Hogarth.

Freud, S. (1908b). Character and anal eroticism. *S. E., 9*: 167–177. London: Hogarth.

Freud, S. (1909d). Notes upon a case of obsessional neurosis. *S. E., 10*: 153–320. London: Hogarth.

Freud, S. (1912b). The dynamics of transference. *S. E., 12*: 99–108. London: Hogarth.

Freud, S. (1912–13). *Totem and Taboo. S. E., 13*: 1–161. London: Hogarth.

Freud, S. (1914c). On narcissism: An introduction. *S. E., 12*: 67–102. London: Hogarth.

Freud, S. (1915b). Thoughts for the times on war and death. *S. E., 14*: 275–299. London: Hogarth.

Freud, S. (1915c). Instincts and their vicissitudes. *S. E., 14*: 117–140. London: Hogarth.

Freud, S. (1916d). Some character-types met with in psychoanalytic work. *S. E., 14*: 316–331. London: Hogarth.

Freud, S. (1918b). From the history of an infantile neurosis. *S. E., 17*: 1–124. London: Hogarth.

Freud, S. (1919h). The "Uncanny". *S. E., 17*: 217–252. London: Hogarth.

Freud, S. (1923b). *The Ego and the Id. S. E., 19*: 3–48. London: Hogarth.

Freud, S. (1924c). The economic problem of masochism. *S. E., 19*: 159–170. London: Hogarth.

Freud, S. (1930a). *Civilization and its Discontents. S. E., 21*: 64–145. London: Hogarth.

Gallwey, P. (1978). *Symbolic dysfunction in the perversions: some related clinical problems*. Unpublished paper.

Gardiner, M. (Ed.) (1972). *The Wolf-Man and Sigmund Freud*. London: Hogarth.

Glasser, M. (1979). Some aspects of the role of aggression in the perversions. In: I. Rosen (Ed.), *Sexual Deviations* (2nd edn) (pp. 278–305). Oxford: Oxford University Press.

Glasser, M. (1986). Identification and its vicissitudes as observed in the perversions. *International Journal of Psychoanalysis, 67*: 9–17.

Glasser, M. (1988). Psychodynamic aspects of paedophilia. *Psychoanalytic Psychotherapy, 3*: 121–135.

Green, A. (1995). Has sexuality anything to do with psychoanalysis? *International Journal of Psychoanalysis, 76*: 871–883.

Green, A. (2000). *The Chains of Eros* (trans. Luke Thurston). London: Rebus.

Green, A. (2002). The central phobic position: A new formulation of the free association method. In: P. Williams (Ed.), *Key Papers on the Borderline* (pp. 49–82). London: Karnac.

Greenson, R. (1970). The exceptional position of the dream in psychoanalytic practice. In: *Explorations in Psychoanalysis* (pp. 387–414). New York: International University Press, 1978.

Guntrip, H. (1961). *Personality Structure and Human Interaction*. London: Hogarth.

Hauptman, J. (1964). *Beyond the Visible: The Art of Odilon Redon*. New York: The Museum of Modern Art.

Hegel, G. W. F. (1964). *The Phenomenology of Mind*. London: George Allen & Unwin.

Hinshelwood, R. D. (2009). *Narcissism and the "Deeper Layers"*. Paper presented at the IPA Congress, Chicago.

Hobbs, R. (1977). *Odilon Redon*. London: Cassell & Collier Macmillan.

Horney, K. (2007). The problem of the negative therapeutic reaction. *Psychoanalytic Quarterly, 76*: 27–42.

Johnson, T. (1993). *Hysteria*. London: Bloomsbury.

Jones, E. (1916). The theory of symbolism. In: *Papers on Psycho-Analysis* (pp. 87–144). London: Baillière, Tindall and Cox, 1948.

Jones, E. (1927). The early development of female sexuality. *International Journal of Psychoanalysis, 8*: 459–472.

Joseph, B. (1971). A clinical contribution to the analysis of a perversion. *International Journal of Psychoanalysis, 52*: 441–449.

Joseph, B. (1983). On understanding and not understanding: Some technical issues. *International Journal of Psychoanalysis, 61*: 291–298.

Joseph, B. (2005). Centre for Advanced Psychoanalytic Studies (CAPS) Lecture, Institute of Psychoanalysis, London.

Jung, C. G. (1969). *On the Nature of the Psyche*. London and New York: Routledge.

Khan, M. (1976). The changing use of dreams in psychoanalytic practice: In search of the dreaming experience. *International Journal of Psychoanalysis, 57*: 325–330.

Khan, M. (1979). *Alienation in Perversions*. London: Hogarth.

Kirshner, L. (1991). The concept of the self in psychoanalytic theory and its philosophical foundations. *Journal of the American Psychoanalytic Association, 39*: 157–182.

Klein, M. (1930). The importance of symbol formation in the development of the ego. In: *Love, Guilt and Reparation and Other Work 1921–1945* (pp. 219–232). London: Hogarth, 1975 [reprinted London: Karnac, 1992].

Klein, M. (1932). *The Psychoanalysis of Children*. London: Hogarth.

Klein, M. (1935). A contribution to the psychogenesis of manic-depressive states. In: *Love, Guilt and Reparation and Other Work 1921–1945* (pp. 262–289). London: Hogarth, 1975. Reprinted by Karnac, London, 1992.

Klein, M. (1940). Mourning and its relation to manic-depressive states. In: *Love, Guilt and Reparation and Other Work 1921–1945* (pp. 344–369). London: Hogarth, 1975. Reprinted by Karnac, London, 1992.

Klein, M. (1946). Notes on some schizoid mechanisms. In: *Envy and Gratitude and Other Works 1946–1963* (pp. 1–24). London: Vintage, 1997.

Klein, M. (1952). The origins of transference. In: *Envy and Gratitude and Other Works 1946–1963* (pp. 48–56). London: Vintage, 1997.

Klein, M. (1957). Envy and gratitude. In: *Envy and Gratitude and Other Works 1946–1963* (pp. 176–235). London: Vintage, 1997.

Klein, M. (1963a). Some Reflections on *The Oresteia*. In: *Envy and Gratitude and Other Works 1946–1963* (pp. 275–299). London: Vintage, 1997.

Klein, M. (1963b). On the sense of loneliness. In: *Envy and Gratitude and Other Works 1946–1963* (pp. 300–313*)*. London: Vintage, 1997.

Kristeva, J. (2001). *Melanie Klein*. New York: Columbia University Press.

Laplanche, J. (1989). Towards a general theory of seduction. In: *New Foundations for Psychoanalysis* (trans. D. Macey) (pp. 104–116). Oxford: Blackwell.

Laplanche, J. (1997). The theory of seduction and the problem of the other. *International Journal of Psychoanalysis, 78*: 653–666.

McDougall, J. (1972). Primal scene and sexual perversion. *International Journal of Psychoanalysis, 53*: 371–384.

McDougall, J. (1995). The Many Faces of Eros: A Psychoanalytic Exploration of Human Sexuality. New York: W. W. Norton.

Meltzer, D. (1967). *The Psycho-Analytic Process*. London: Heinemann.

Meltzer, D. (1973). *Sexual States of Mind*. Perth: Clunie.

Meltzer, D. (1981). The Kleinian expansion of Freudian metapsychology. *International Journal of Psychoanalysis, 62*: 177–185.

Meltzer, D. (1983). *Dream-Life*. Perth: Clunie.

Mills, J. (2000). Hegel on projective identification: Implications for Klein, Bion and Beyond. *Psychoanalytic Review, 87*: 841–874.

Milner, M. (1969). *The Hands of the Living God*. London: Hogarth.

Modell, A. (1965). On having the right to a life: An aspect of the superego's development. *International Journal of Psychoanalysis, 46*: 323–331.

M'Uzan, M. de (2010). The Uncanny, or "I am not who you think I am". In: D. Birksted-Breen, S. Flanders, & A. Gibeault (Ed.), *Reading French Psychoanalysis* (pp. 201–209). London and New York: Routledge.

Nettleton, S. (2015). *The Metapsychology of Christopher Bollas: An Introduction*. London and New York: Routledge.

O'Shaughnessy, E. (1999). Relating to the Superego. *International Journal of Psychoanalysis, 80*: 861–870.

Padel, J. (1987). Personal communication.

Perelberg, R. (2015). *Murdered Father, Dead Father: Revisiting the Oedipus Complex*. London: New Library of Psychoanalysis.

Rey, H. (1994). *Universals of Psychoanalysis in the Treatment of Psychotic and Borderline States*. London: Free Association.

Riesenberg-Malcolm, R. (1981). Expiation as a defence. *International Journal of Psychoanalytic Psychotherapy, 8*: 549–570.

Riviere, J. (1936). A contribution to the analysis of the negative therapeutic reaction. *International Journal of Psychoanalysis, 17*: 304–320.

Rosenberg, V. (2011). Sexuality and the analytic couple. In: J. Arundale & D. Bellman (Eds.), *Transference and Countertransference: A Unifying Focus of Psychoanalysis*. London: Karnac.

Rosenfeld, H. (1965). *Psychotic States: A Psychoanalytic Approach*. London: Hogarth.

Rosenfeld, H. (1971). A clinical approach to the psychoanalytic theory of the life and death instincts: An investigation into the aggressive aspects of narcissism. *International Journal of Psychoanalysis, 52*: 169–178.

Rosenfeld, H. (1985). *Psychotic States: A Psychoanalytical Approach.* London: Karnac.

Rosenfeld, H. (1987). *Impasse and Interpretation.* London: Routledge.

Rosenfeld, H. (2008). *Rosenfeld in Retrospect* (ed. J. Steiner). London and New York: Routledge.

Roth, P. (2003). Verbal communication.

Rusbridger, R. (2004). Elements of the Oedipus complex: A Kleinian account. *International Journal of Psychoanalysis, 85*: 731–747.

Rycroft, C. (1979). *The Innocence of Dreams.* London: Hogarth.

Sandler, J. (1983). Reflections on some relations between psychoanalytic concepts and psychoanalytic practice. *International Journal of Psychoanalysis, 64*: 35–45.

Sandler, J. (1987). The concept of projective identification. *Bulletin of the Anna Freud Centre, 10*: 33–49.

Sandler, J., & Sandler, A-M. (1987). The past unconscious, the present unconscious and the vicissitudes of guilt. *International Journal of Psychoanalysis, 68*: 331–341.

Schafer, R. (1997). Blocked introjection/blocked incorporation. In: D. Bell (Ed.), *Reason and Passion: A Celebration of the Work of Hannah Segal* (pp. 139–146). London: Duckworth.

Segal, H. (1957). Notes on symbol formation. In: *The Work of Hanna Segal.* London: Free Association & Maresfield, 1986.

Segal, H, (1986). *The Work of Hanna Segal.* London: Free Association & Maresfield.

Segal, H. (2007). Psychic structure and psychic change. In: N. Abel-Hirsch (Ed.), *Yesterday, Today and Tomorrow* (pp. 83–91). London: Routledge.

Sharpe, E. (1937). *Dream Analysis.* London: Hogarth.

Sodré, I. (2015). "The perpetual orgy": Hysterical phantasies, bisexuality and the question of bad faith. In: *Imaginary Existences* (pp. 216–231). London: Routledge.

Sohn, L. (1998). Verbal communication.

Spillius, E. (2007). *Encounters with Melanie Klein: Selected Papers of Elizabeth Spillius.* London and New York: Routledge.

Spillius, E., Milton, J., Garvey, P., Couve, C., & Steiner, D. (2011). *The New Dictionary of Kleinian Thought.* London and New York: Routledge.

Stein, R. (2003). *Sexuality Psychoanalytically Conceived.* Paper presented at the 25th International Anna Freud Centre Colloquium, London: Has sex left psychoanalysis?

Steiner, J. (1993). *Psychic Retreats.* London: Karnac.

Stoller, R. (1976). *Perversion: The Erotic Form of Hatred*. Brighton: Harvester [reprinted London: Karnac, 1986.]

Vermote, R. (2011). Bion's critical approach to psychoanalysis. In: C. Mawson (Ed.), *Bion Today* (pp. 345–369). London: Routledge.

Welldon, E. (1996). Perversions in men and women. *British Journal of Psychotherapy, 12*: 480–486.

Werner, A. (1969). *The Graphic Works of Odilon Redon*. New York: Dover.

Williams, G. (1997). Reflections on some dynamics of eating disorders: "No entry" defences and foreign bodies. *International Journal of Psychoanalysis, 78*: 927–941.

Winnicott, D. W. (1965). *The Maturational Processes and the Facilitating Environment: Studies in the Theory of Emotional Development*. London: Hogarth.

Winnicott, D. W. (1969). The use of an object. *International Journal of Psychoanalysis, 50*: 711–716.

INDEX